# THE ULTIMATE BOOK OF SCIENCE

## Everything you need to know

# OXFORD
UNIVERSITY PRESS

Great Clarendon Street, Oxford OX2 6DP

Oxford University Press is a department of the University of Oxford.
It furthers the University's objective of excellence in research,
scholarship, and education by publishing worldwide in

Oxford   New York

Auckland   Cape Town   Dar es Salaam   Hong Kong   Karachi
Kuala Lumpur   Madrid   Melbourne   Mexico City   Nairobi
New Delhi   Shanghai   Taipei   Toronto

With offices in

Argentina   Austria   Brazil   Chile   Czech Republic   France   Greece
Guatemala   Hungary   Italy   Japan   Poland   Portugal   Singapore
South Korea   Switzerland   Thailand   Turkey   Ukraine   Vietnam

Oxford is a registered trade mark of Oxford University Press
in the UK and in certain other countries

British Library Cataloguing in Publication Data

Data available

ISBN 978 0 19 911977-6

10 9 8 7 6 5 4 3 2 1

Originated by Oxford University Press

Created by White-Thomson Publishing Ltd

Printed in China

2

# Contents

## PLANET EARTH

## CLIMATE, WEATHER, AND THE ENVIRONMENT

## HUMAN BODIES

## PLANTS AND ANIMALS

## SPACE

## PHYSICS AND HOW OUR WORLD WORKS

## CHEMICALS AND HOW THEY BEHAVE

## MATERIALS AND STRUCTURES

## TECHNOLOGY AND MACHINES

## INDUSTRY AND TRANSPORT

# The Earth

The Earth is a rocky planet that orbits (travels around) the Sun. From space, the Earth looks blue. This is because 70 per cent of its surface is covered with water.

Unlike any other planet that we know, the Earth is home to millions of different kinds of living things.

The Earth from space, showing clouds over the continent of South America.

## Moving through space

The Earth is constantly moving through space. It is about 150 million kilometres (93 million miles) from the Sun. The journey around the Sun takes a year – just over 365 days.

As it orbits, the Earth spins once each day. On the side of the Earth facing the Sun it is day. The side facing away from the Sun is in shadow, and it is night.

## Formation of the Earth

The Sun, the Earth and other planets formed around 4.5 billion years ago from a cloud of dust and gas.

1. The Solar System (the Sun and the planets that orbit the Sun) began as a cloud of gas and dust.

2. Most of the gas and dust formed the Sun. Around the Sun the planets formed. One of these planets was the Earth.

3. At first, the Earth was so hot that its surface was almost all molten (fluid).

4. Over time, the Earth cooled. An outer crust of hard rock formed. Water vapour in the air condensed (changed from a gas to a liquid) to form oceans.

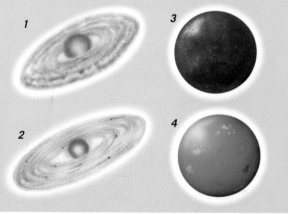

This is what the Earth would look like without oceans hiding the ocean floor. There are high mountain ranges, deep valleys and flat plains both on the ocean floor and on the continents.

## Seasons

The Earth is tilted on its axis (an imaginary line that passes between the poles). For half of the year, the North Pole leans towards the Sun. For the other half of the year, the South Pole leans towards the Sun. This tilt gives the Earth its seasons. It is summer in the part of the Earth tilted towards the Sun.

## The life zone

The Earth is at just the right temperature for life to exist. It has liquid water on its surface and gases in the air. The air surrounding the Earth is called the atmosphere.

Animals need oxygen in the atmosphere to breathe and water to drink. Plants need water and carbon dioxide gas, which is also found in the atmosphere.

### FAST FACTS

**The Earth's atmosphere contains**:
- ☐ Nitrogen (78 per cent)
- ☐ Oxygen (21 per cent)
- ☐ Argon (0.93 per cent)
- ☐ Carbon dioxide (0.04 per cent)

◀ These lights in the atmosphere are seen in the far north and far south. They are caused by particles from the Sun hitting the Earth's atmosphere.

## Inside the Earth

The Earth is made of five different layers – the atmosphere, crust, mantle, outer core and inner core.

1. The inner core is made mostly of iron. It is even hotter than the outer core. The weight of the rocks above push down on it. This makes the inner core solid instead of liquid.

2. The outer core is made of hot fluid iron. Scientists think that the iron liquid moves around slowly inside the core.

3. The mantle is made of solid rock. It is much hotter than the outer crust and the rocks are tightly packed.

4. The crust is the rocky outer layer of the Earth. We live on the crust and the oceans rest on it.

5. The atmosphere is the layer of gas surrounding the Earth.

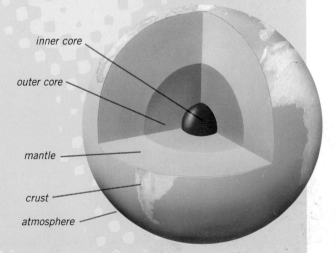

inner core

outer core

mantle

crust

atmosphere

# Air

You are surrounded by gases. You can't see them, and you can't smell them. But you can feel them move in and out of your body as you breathe.

When the wind blows you can feel the gases brush against your skin. The mixture of gases is called air.

When the wind blows, the air can push along sailing boats.

## The atmosphere

Air surrounds the Earth in a thick layer called the atmosphere. Air contains mostly nitrogen (78 per cent) and oxygen (21 per cent). It also contains smaller amounts of other gases, including carbon dioxide.

If the air inside a balloon is heated, it becomes less dense (more spaced out) than the surrounding air. This makes it rise and lift the balloon.

## Air for living things

Humans and other animals need to breathe in oxygen to make their bodies work. Without oxygen we would die. We breathe out another gas, carbon dioxide.

Plants need carbon dioxide. They use carbon dioxide, water and the power of the Sun to make their own food. As they do so, they give out oxygen.

## Air pressure

The atmosphere is hundreds of kilometres thick. This means that there is a lot of air pressing down on us. At sea level, there is a force of about 1 kilogram (2.2 pounds) pressing on every square centimetre (0.2 square inches) of your body. This force is called air pressure.

At sea level, the weight of air is about 1 kilogram (2.2 pounds) for every square centimetre (0.2 square inches). As you go higher in the atmosphere, the air pressure gets lower.

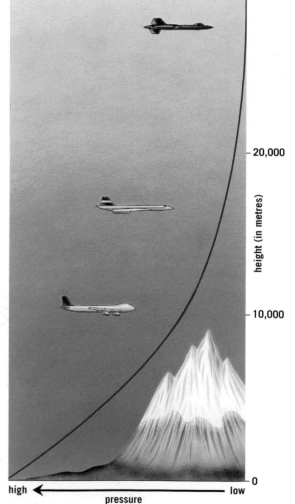

30,000

20,000

height (in metres)

10,000

0

high ← → low

pressure

# Rocks and geology

Rocks are all around you. They are the natural, solid parts of the Earth. You can see rocks at the coast, on cliff faces and in the ground.

Most rocks are made of substances called minerals. Some rocks are made of plants and animals that died millions of years ago. Geology is the study of rocks and the structure of the Earth.

## Igneous rock

Igneous rock forms when hot molten rock from inside the Earth cools and becomes solid. Granite and basalt are igneous rocks.

## Sedimentary rock

Sedimentary rock forms from sediments (tiny pieces of rock). Sediments are carried by rivers and eventually settle on the sea floor.

Over millions of years they are squashed by more layers of sediment. They become rocks. Limestone and sandstone are sedimentary rocks.

**FAST FACTS**

☐ There are more than 2,500 types of mineral.
☐ Gold, silver, quartz, diamonds and rubies are minerals

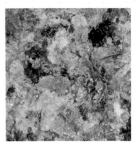 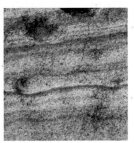

Granite forms deep underground when hot, fluid rocks cool and harden. It is an igneous rock.

Sandstone is a sedimentary rock. It is made of small grains of sand that settled and have been squashed together.

## Metamorphic rock

Sometimes, igneous and sedimentary rock heat up under great pressure. They change into metamorphic rock.

When limestone is squashed underground where it is hot, it forms a metamorphic rock called marble.

How different rock types form.

weathering and transport by wind and rain

sediments carried by wind and rivers

cooling lava forms igneous rock

sediments dumped in the sea

layers of sedimentary rock

sedimentary rocks on seabed

igneous rocks inside the Earth

heat and pressure form metamorphic rocks

## Learning from rocks

People who study rocks are called geologists. Geologists use clues from rocks to learn about the Earth's history.

To a geologist, a piece of sandstone is not just a rock. It is part of an ancient beach or desert. Its sand particles were once part of a mountain. The sandstone might contain the bones of an extinct animal, or it could have imprints of an ancient plant.

## Detective work

A geologist is a bit like a detective. They look closely at rivers and rock formations. They study minerals under a microscope. They gather evidence and use it to form ideas about how the Earth formed. They also try to find out how the Earth may change in the future.

### DID YOU KNOW?

Rocks tell us what a place was like millions of years ago. They show us what the weather was like, which animals and plants were alive, and whether it was desert or swamp, land or sea, mountains or plains.

## What do geologists do?

Geologists:

- study volcanoes so that they can predict eruptions.
- look for important minerals like copper and gold.
- make sure rocks are stable enough to build on.
- look for water underground.
- study rocks to find out how the Earth formed.

**This geologist is studying a recent lava flow from a volcano.**

# Fossils

Fossils are the preserved remains of living things that died millions of years ago. There are many kinds of fossil. Some fossils formed from live plants or animals, such as a woolly mammoth's skeleton. Other fossils are signs of living things that were once alive, such as dinosaur tracks or leaf prints.

The fossil of an ammonite, nearly 200 million years old. Ammonites were shelled sea creatures that became extinct at the same time as the dinosaurs.

## Fossil formation

It usually takes thousands or millions of years for a fossil to form. Here you can see how a sea creature becomes a fossil.

1. The creature dies and settles to the sea floor.

2. It is covered by sediments (particles of mud and sand). The flesh rots away, but the skeleton remains.

3. The sediments harden to form rock. The skeleton gets squashed and broken.

4. Earth movements lift up the rock layers. The sea level drops.

5. Wind and rain wears away the rocks. The fossil of the skeleton is revealed.

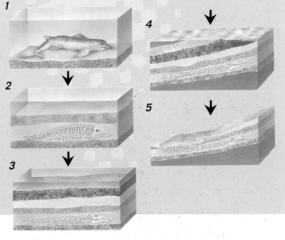

**DID YOU KNOW?**

*In CE 79, Mount Vesuvius exploded. Hot ash buried the city of Pompeii in Italy. People and their animals burned. Imprints of their bodies were left in the ash. In hours, thousands of people became fossils preserved in rock.*

## Fossils tell a story

Fossils show us what life was like on Earth in prehistoric times. They show us which animals and plants were alive. They can also show us what the ground was made of at different times in the Earth's history.

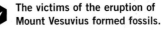

The victims of the eruption of Mount Vesuvius formed fossils.

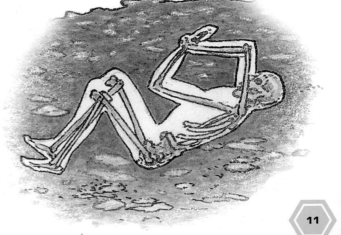

# Crystals

Crystals are all around us. Digital watches, diamond rings and gold bars all contain crystals.

Everything is made up of tiny particles called atoms and molecules. The particles in crystals are arranged in a regular, repeating pattern.

## Regular shapes

The pattern of a crystal's particles is repeated over and over again. This gives crystals regular (in a fixed pattern) shapes.

Crystals have many different regular shapes, such as cubes, pyramids, hexagons and prisms.

◀ Quartz crystals are found in the Earth's crust.

Diamonds are hard, valuable crystals. ⬢▶

## Colours

Lots of pure crystals, such as salt and sugar crystals, are white or transparent. Other crystals are coloured. Rubies are red and sapphires are usually blue.

## Large and small

Some crystals are large and can be seen clearly. Diamond and quartz are large crystals. Other crystals are small.

You can see the crystalline shape of table salt if you look at it through a magnifying glass. In metal, the crystals are even smaller. You can only see them through a powerful microscope.

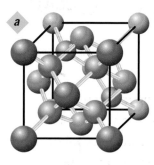

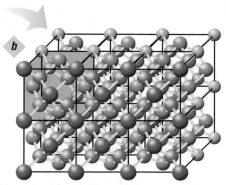

Fluorite is a crystal found in rocks. Its particles are arranged in a cube-shaped repeating pattern (a and b). Fluorite crystals have the 14-sided shape shown here (c).

# Caves

Caves are natural underground rooms and passages. Some are small, but others are huge. They can have chambers the size of cathedrals. Undergound passages can extend for many kilometres.

## Limestone caves

The most common kinds of cave are limestone caves. Limestone is a type of rock. Water seeps through cracks in the limestone. Over time, acidic water dissolves and washes away the limestone. A cave forms.

## Towering limestone

The limestone pinnacles (peaks) in the photograph below are all that is left of a thick layer of limestone. Over millions of years, water, which is acidic, has dissolved away the rest of the rock. There are small caves inside the pinnacles.

These limestone peaks are in China.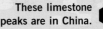

Rainwater seeps through cracks in the limestone and slowly dissolves away the rock. This forms caves.

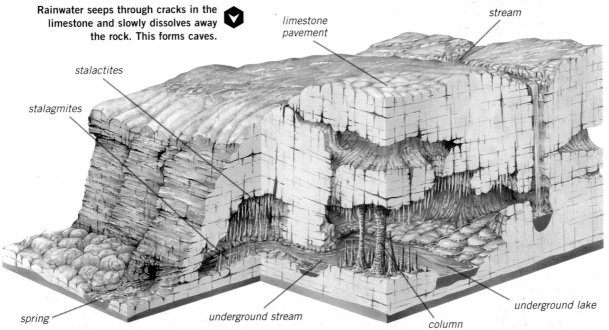

stalactites

stalagmites

limestone pavement

stream

spring

underground stream

column

underground lake

## Others kinds of cave

There are several kinds of cave. Sea caves form where waves pound a cliff. The water slowly carves a hole in the rock. A river flowing through a glacier can carve out an ice cave.

Lava tube caves form near volcanoes. As a river of lava (hot, molten rock) flows, its surface cools and turns solid. The lava inside stays warm and keeps flowing. When the liquid lava drains away, it leaves an empty cave behind.

# Earthquakes

Earthquakes make the ground shake violently. This movement can destroy towns and cities.

Earthquakes happen because of movements in the Earth's surface, or crust. The crust is made of many large pieces, called plates. The plates move very slowly. Most earthquakes happen at the edges of these plates.

The line in these rocks shows where two of the Earth's plates meet. This line is in the United States and is called the San Andreas fault line.

## Earth's plates

In some places, the Earth's plates rub past each other all the time. Tiny earthquakes, called tremors, happen every day in these places.

In other parts of the world, the plates get stuck as they try to move past one another. They can get stuck for many years. When they eventually move, they produce a massive earthquake.

A powerful earthquake has destroyed this town, Golcuk, in Turkey.

This map shows where strong earthquakes have happened in recent years. It also shows how deep the earthquakes happened inside the Earth's crust.

## Shockwaves

When an earthquake happens, the rocks of the Earth's surface move suddenly. Some rocks move from side to side. Others move up and down, or are squeezed and stretched.

The movement sends shock waves out in all directions. The shock waves are what shake the ground and buildings during an earthquake.

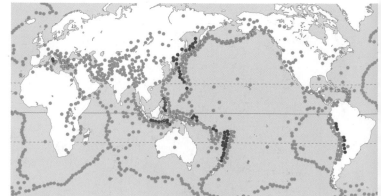

**Earthquake depths:**

■ less than 70 km (43 miles)
■ 70 to 300 km (43 to 186 miles)
■ 300 to 700 km (186 to 435 miles)

# Volcanoes

Lava, hot ash and gases spew from volcanoes. The Earth's surface, or crust, floats on a layer of hot, molten rock (magma). Sometimes, the molten rock finds its way to the surface, and bursts through. A volcano forms.

Lava from a volcano can flow over huge areas of land, destroying anything in its path.

**DID YOU KNOW?**

Hot flows of lava, steam and rock can race out of a volcano at 100 kilometres (62 miles) per hour.

A volcano erupting in Hawaii. The lava is so hot that it glows.

## What is a volcano?

A volcano is a place where magma erupts onto the surface of the Earth; it is then called lava. At first, the lava is liquid. As it runs down the side of the volcano, the lava cools and hardens.

**FAST FACTS**

☐ Magma is molten rock that is underground.

☐ Lava is molten rock that is above the ground.

## Eruptions

The inside of the Earth is very hot. Some of the heat escapes through volcanic eruptions. This helps the Earth to cool down. Eruptions can be calm or they can be explosive. Volcanoes that contain runny magma have calm eruptions. Volcanoes that contain thick, sticky magma explode violently. They send hot lava, ash and gases high up into the air, which rain down on the surrounding area. Both types of eruptions can cause a lot of damage.

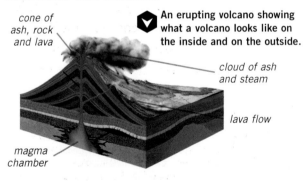

cone of ash, rock and lava

An erupting volcano showing what a volcano looks like on the inside and on the outside.

cloud of ash and steam

lava flow

magma chamber

## Types of volcano

Some volcanoes have steep sides made of layers of lava and ash. They are steep because the lava is thick and sticky. The lava cannot travel very far before it hardens. Other volcanoes are wide and have gentle slopes. The lava that erupts from these volcanoes is very runny. It flows a long way from the volcano before it hardens.

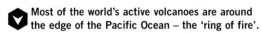
Most of the world's active volcanoes are around the edge of the Pacific Ocean – the 'ring of fire'.

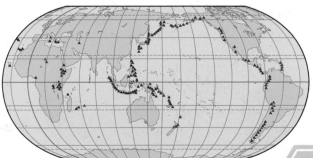

# Deserts

Deserts can be hot or cold. The one thing they all have in common is that they are dry.

In fact, deserts are the driest places on Earth. They have less than 25 centimetres (10 inches) of rain each year.

## Desert landscape

Winds blow sand into sand dunes. The dunes move constantly. But not all deserts are sandy. Many of them are rocky. Two-thirds of the Sahara Desert is rocky, not sandy.

An oasis is a place in the desert where there is surface water. Trees and plants grow in an oasis.

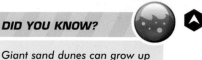

**DID YOU KNOW?**

*Giant sand dunes can grow up to 150 metres (490 feet) high.*

Sand dunes in the Sahara Desert. Sand dunes can move up to 30 metres (98 feet) in a year.

## Hot and cold deserts

The world's largest deserts, such as the Sahara Desert, are hot. They are found near the tropics. Cold deserts are found near the Poles of the Earth.

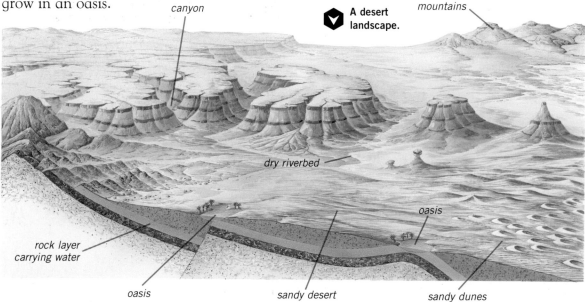

A desert landscape.

canyon

mountains

dry riverbed

oasis

rock layer carrying water

oasis

sandy desert

sandy dunes

**DID YOU KNOW?**

The driest deserts on Earth are the cold, dry valleys of Antarctica.

## Desert formation

Deserts form when the air above them is very dry. Water in the oceans evaporates (turns from a liquid into a gas or vapour). It rises into the air and makes clouds. But deserts are often far from the oceans. By the time the air reaches a distant desert, it has lost most of its water vapour as rain.

# Forests

Forest are large areas of tree-covered land. Different kinds of forest grow in different climates.

All forests provide habitats for plants and animals. They also provide humans with wood, paper, food and medicines.

**DID YOU KNOW?**

At least half of all the animal and plant species in the world live in rainforests.

Some rainforest plants such as orchids, ferns, mosses and bromeliads grow high on the tree branches.

## Rainforests

Rainforests grow near the Equator. It is hot and wet in a rainforest all year round. The canopy (tree tops) receive lots of rain and sunshine.

The trees are bursting with life. Thousands of different insects, birds and animals live on the leaves, flowers and fruits of the rainforest trees.

In autumn, deciduous forests look red and gold. The leaves dry up and fall off the trees.

## Cooler forests

Deciduous forests grow further away from the Equator. They need warm summers, cool winters and rainfall. Deciduous trees lose their leaves in winter.

Coniferous forests grow in cooler, drier regions across the north of the Earth. Conifers have needles instead of broad leaves to reduce water loss. They do not lose their leaves in winter.

## Surviving the seasons

In deciduous and coniferous forests, spring and summer are times for plants to grow and flower. Animals have their young. In autumn, nuts and berries ripen on the trees. Animals feast or store food for the winter. In winter, some birds and mammals migrate, travelling to warmer places to find more food.

To survive the cold winter, dormice go into a deep sleep called hibernation. They use the fat stored in their bodies to survive.

17

# Grasslands

Grasslands are very wide, open grassy areas. Grasslands grow in places where it is too dry for forests but too wet for deserts. They are home to grazing animals such as antelopes and buffalo.

Natural grasslands exist in parts of Africa, North America, South America and Asia. In many areas, grasslands have been ploughed up and used to grow crops.

## Grass

Grasses are tough plants. Grazing animals chew the grasses almost down to the ground. Most grasses grow thicker and faster after being eaten. They also grow back well after fires.

In dry or cold seasons, grasses die back completely above the ground. Animals may have to travel long distances to find enough food and water.

This cheetah has just made a kill on the African savannah (grassland).

## Insects

Hordes of tiny insects, such as beetles, ants, grasshoppers and caterpillars, live in grasslands. Because there are so many of them, insects can eat far more than the big grazers.

Termites and dung beetles help to turn animal dung and the remains of dead plants and animals into rich soil.

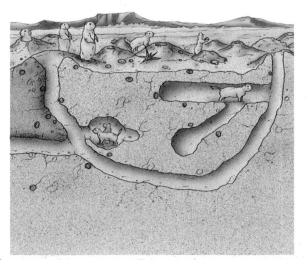

Prairie dogs dig tunnels under the North American prairies (grasslands). They do this to escape predators and shelter from bad weather.

**DID YOU KNOW?**

*Locusts are insects. They eat grass. A large swarm of locusts can eat as much food in a day as 10 elephants or 2,500 people.*

Locusts and other insects feed on grass.

# Mountains

Mountains are high peaks of land. They form over millions of years as the Earth's surface changes. They are shaped by the wind, rain and ice.

## How mountains form

The Earth's surface is made of separate plates (large, rigid pieces) that fit together like a jigsaw. The plates move constantly. Mountains form as the plates move.

There are four main kinds of mountains: fold mountains, thrust mountains, fault block mountains and volcanic mountains. Volcanic mountains form where molten rock erupts on the Earth's surface.

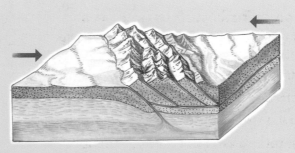

Thrust mountains form where two land masses slowly crash into each other. The land crumples up into mountains.

Fold mountains form where the top layers of rock are worn away. The folded mountains underneath are revealed.

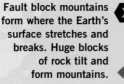

Fault block mountains form where the Earth's surface stretches and breaks. Huge blocks of rock tilt and form mountains.

## Shaping mountains

Mountains are shaped by running water, wind and ice. Tall jagged mountains are worn away over millions of years. Many ancient mountain ranges are now just low hills or flat lands.

**DID YOU KNOW?**

*In the past, the Highlands of Scotland were as tall and jagged as the Alps. They have been gradually worn away.*

These mountain peaks formed deep underground. The rocks above them slowly wore away. Glaciers have carved the rock into sharp peaks.

# Ice caps and glaciers

Ice caps and glaciers are thick masses of ice that flow over land. They can form anywhere that is very cold and snowy.

They can be as small as a few hundred metres across, or as large as a continent.

## Rock made of ice

Some snow that falls in the winter doesn't completely melt in the summer. Instead it gradually piles up year after year. The snow becomes tightly packed and turns into solid ice.

The pile of ice and snow can get so thick that it starts to flow. A glacier has formed.

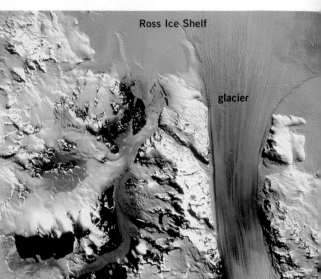

Ross Ice Shelf

glacier

This satellite photo over Antarctica shows a large glacier on the right hand side. It is flowing from the coast into the permanently frozen Ross Ice Shelf (top).

## Flowing rock

Gravity makes glaciers flow. Glaciers on mountains flow downhill. Ice sheets on flatter land spread outwards. Glaciers move between a few centimetres and a few metres every day.

Glaciers shape landscapes. As the glacier moves, the ice scrapes away the rock beneath it and on either side.

surrounding land

glacier

## Antarctica

Most of Antarctica is covered in ice. Its ice sheets can be 3 kilometres (1.9 miles) thick. The ice sheets flow very slowly from the centre of Antarctica out towards the sea. Huge chunks break off into icebergs that float out to sea. Climate change is warming the Earth. More and more glaciers and ice caps are melting.

Glaciers melt as they near the sea. Huge icebergs break off and float away.

# Oceans and coasts

The Earth has five oceans that are all connected together. These are the Atlantic, Pacific, Indian, Arctic and Southern oceans. Together they cover almost three-quarters of the Earth's surface.

A coast is where the land meets the sea or ocean. Coasts can be sandy, rocky or muddy. All coasts are constantly changing.

Waves in the oceans are caused by the wind. Very strong winds can form enormous waves.

## Currents

Ocean water flows around the Earth in great rivers called currents. The wind drives currents on the ocean's surface. Other currents flow downwards from the surface. These currents travel along deep in the ocean.

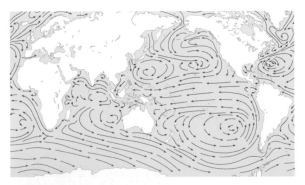

## Salt water

Ocean water is salty because it is full of minerals. Rocks contain minerals. Rivers wash the minerals off the land and into the oceans. The main mineral in ocean water is sodium chloride. This is the same mineral that we sprinkle on food – table salt.

 This map shows the surface currents in the oceans. Red arrows show currents of warm water. Blue arrows show currents of cold water.

**DID YOU KNOW?**

If you removed the minerals from the oceans, they would form a layer of salt 50 metres (164 feet) thick.

## The ocean floor

The rocky crust beneath the ocean is about 10 kilometres (6 miles) thick. On top of the rocks is a layer of clay and mud.

In some places, ocean water is heated by hot rocks beneath the ocean floor. These hot springs contain minerals that feed the deep ocean animals.

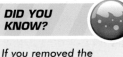 A hot spring on the ocean floor is sometimes called a black smoker.

Atolls are coral islands. The coral (tiny underwater animals) grows on the cones of underwater volcanoes. Atolls often have sandy coasts.

## Types of coasts

Some coasts are sandy, with soft, wide beaches. Some are muddy areas at the mouth of a river. Other coasts are lined with boulders and pebbles.

In some places the land slopes gradually towards the ocean. In others it drops off suddenly into the ocean with a steep cliff.

## Changing coasts

Coastlines change over time. The ocean wears away rocks from one part of the coast and then moves them to another. Waves hammer at cliffs and wear them away.

## Sinking and rising

Some coasts are actually sinking into the sea. Others are rising up out of it. During an ice age, the land is covered with ice. The ice pushes down on the land. The land tilts into the seas and oceans. When the ice melts, the land moves up again.

**DID YOU KNOW?**

During powerful earthquakes, the coasts of California, Japan and the Mediterranean have been pushed up out of the ocean.

Over millions of years, a hilly coast with cliffs and boulders can change into a wide, gently sloping sandy beach.

The shape of a coastline is affected by waves and currents.

*rivers dump mud*

*wide, sandy beaches shaped by waves*

*sea wears away cliffs*

*arch*

*pillar*

*sand or pebbles pile up to form long ridges called spits*

*ocean currents transport sand and mud down the coast*

# Rivers and lakes

When rain falls on land, it trickles over the ground. Trickles of water join together to form streams. Eventually, these streams come together and form rivers.

Rivers flow until they empty into the sea or a lake. A lake forms when water gathers in a hollow.

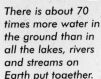

**DID YOU KNOW?**

There is about 70 times more water in the ground than in all the lakes, rivers and streams on Earth put together.

## Rivers

The water at the beginning of a river flows quickly. Further along, the water slows down. As the river nears a sea or lake, it dumps mud that it has been carrying. This builds a delta, which is a fan shape of islands and water channels.

Rivers are constantly changing. They can cut deeper channels. They can drop mud to create islands. During a flood, part of a river can jump over to a completely new course.

Rivers change along their course from the mountains to the sea.

rain and snow

glacier

floodplain

delta

ocean

lake

mud, sand and gravel

This lake has formed in the crater of a volcano.

**FAST FACTS**

The world's deepest lake is Lake Baykal in Siberia. It is 630 kilometres (390 miles) long and more than 1,500 metres (4,920 feet) deep.

## Lakes

Lakes form where water collects in a hollow. The hollows can be made in different ways:

**Glacier lakes** – Glaciers carve huge hollows in land.

**Crater lakes** – Volcanoes erupt and can blow off their peaks. A hollow crater forms.

**Rift valley lakes** – The Earth's crust is constantly moving. It can stretch and break, creating huge hollows.

# Wetlands

Marshes, bogs and swamps are types of wetland. The soil in wetlands is either very damp or covered with water. Wetlands provide homes for many plants, animals and birds.

## Wetland plants

Water provides support for wetland plants. The plants do not need strong stems or roots. Many water plants float near the surface to be near the light. Some use the water to spread their pollen and seeds.

A kingfisher dives to catch fish from a wetland. It returns with the fish in its beak. It can make up to 100 dives in one day.

## Important wetlands

Many animals and birds breed in wetlands because there is plenty of food and shelter. Birds also stop to feed and rest on wetlands during long journeys.

Wetlands soak up lots of water. This can help to protect the lands around them from storms and floods.

## Water spiders

Water spiders live underwater in some wetlands. However, they need to breathe air. They spin a dome of silk and fix it to an underwater plant. They fill the dome with bubbles of air. The spider leaves its silk bubble when it needs to collect air or catch food.

The long, narrow hooves of these deer help them to run and leap through swampy ground. They are also good swimmers.

Water spider inside its air bubble.

# Tides

Every day the Earth's seas and oceans slowly rise and fall. These rises and falls are called tides.

If you are on a beach, high tide is when the sea comes in and low tide is when it goes out.

At low tide, a wide beach is revealed. ▶

## Gravity

Tides are caused by gravity. Gravity is the force that attracts one object to another. The gravity of the Moon and the Sun pull on the Earth. This pull causes the tides.

## The pull of the Moon

The Moon orbits (travels round) the Earth. Its gravity pulls on the seawater and makes it bulge. One bulge forms on the side of the Earth facing the Moon. Another bulge forms directly opposite. There are high tides at the two bulges and low tides in between.

Most places on Earth have one high tide and one low tide every day. This is because the Earth is rotating throughout the day.

There are spring tides when the Sun and the Moon are in a line. When they pull in different directions there is less difference between high and low tides. ▶

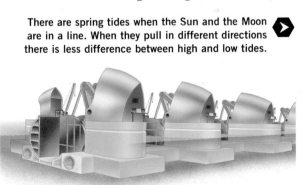

▲ The Thames Barrier protects London from flooding. Otherwise, London could flood if there is a powerful storm at the same time as high tide.

## The pull of the Sun

The Sun also pulls on the water. When the Sun and the Moon are in a line, they both pull on the water. This makes a very high tide called a spring tide.

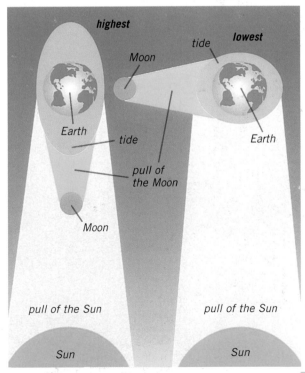

highest

Moon

tide    lowest

Earth

tide

Earth

pull of the Moon

Moon

pull of the Sun

pull of the Sun

Sun

Sun

# Seashores

Where they meet the sea, rivers form flat, muddy areas called estuaries. Birds feed on worms and snails in the mud.

Seashores are places where the ocean or sea meets the land. Seashores can be sandy, muddy, or rocky. Seashore creatures must be able to survive both dry and wet conditions.

## Barnacles

Barnacles are animals that cling to rocks. When barnacles are covered with seawater, their feathery 'legs' stick out from their shells. They use these to catch food in the water. At low tide, barnacles pull their 'legs' inside their shells.

Barnacles have tough shells to protect them from strong waves.

## Life on the seashore

When the tide flows in, the seashore is covered with water. The water contains floating food. Seashore creatures feed on this food.

When the tide flows out, the land is dried by winds and the Sun. Some creatures burrow into the sand or mud to stop themselves drying out. Others, such as shellfish, have tough shells for protection from the weather.

## Rock pools

Rock pools form on rocky seashores. At high tide, water collects in a rocky hollow. When the tide goes out, the pool of water is left behind. It is like a tiny, self-contained world.

Rock-pool plants include tiny algae and larger seaweeds. Winkles and limpets eat the plants. Starfishes, small fishes, and whelks eat the plant-eaters.

Different plants and animals live at different levels on a rocky seashore.

1 sea kelp
2 serrated wrack
3 sea anemone
4 thong weed
5 starfish
6 bladder wrack
7 mussels
8 knotted wrack
9 barnacles
10 spiral wrack
11 channel wrack
12 lichen

# Resources

The Earth's land, air, and oceans contain substances that humans use to make everyday items. We call these substances the Earth's resources.

Oil is one of the most valuable resources. Oil can be made into fuels. It can also be used to make plastics, paints, and other useful substances.

**DID YOU KNOW?**

*Every hour of every day, 500 million litres (132 million gallons) of oil are pumped out of the ground. One day, the oil will run out.*

## Land resources

Limestone is a type of rock. It is used to make cement and concrete for buildings and roads. Beach sand is used to make glass. Clays are used to make bricks and pottery.

Some rocks contain metals. These rocks are called ores. Metals are used to build machines for industry, transport, and our homes.

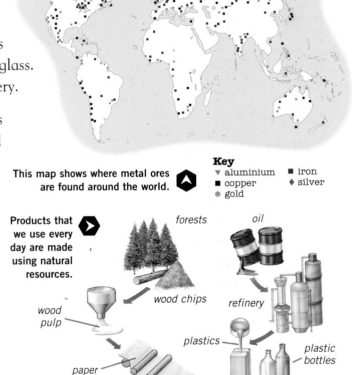

This map shows where metal ores are found around the world.

**Key**
- ▼ aluminium    ■ iron
- ■ copper    ◆ silver
- ● gold

## Ocean and air resources

The oceans are full of salt. Salt has many uses in industry – it is used to make paper, soaps, and dyes.

Air is a mixture of gases, including nitrogen and oxygen. Nitrogen is used to make fertilizers for plants. Oxygen is used in space rockets to help the fuel burn.

Products that we use every day are made using natural resources.

forests

oil

wood chips

refinery

wood pulp

plastics

paper

plastic bottles

## Living resources

Forests provide us with wood for building homes and making paper. Farms give us useful crops such as rubber and cotton. Other crops, such as rape, sunflowers, and flax, are grown for the oil contained in their seeds.

 Rainforests are rich in natural resources, including wood.

# Maps

Road maps help us plan a route from one place to another.

A map is a flat diagram of an area of land, sea, or sky. You can make a map of almost anything, from the anthills in your back garden to the stars in outer space.

Maps contain information about places. Road maps help people to find their way around. Political maps show where countries are in the world.

---

## Reading maps

On most maps, north is towards the top. West is to the left, east to the right, and south to the bottom.

**Land height in metres (feet)**

| | |
|---|---|
| | 2,000–5,000 (6,560–16,400) |
| | 1,000–2,000 (3,280–6,560) |
| | 500–1,000 (1,640–6,560) |
| | 200–500 (660–1,640) |
| | less than 200 (less than 660) |

Different heights of the land are shown in different colours on the map. The key tells you what the different colours mean. The key also explains the meanings of the symbols.

**Key**

| | |
|---|---|
| | country boundary |
| | province boundary |
| ◆ | capital |
| ■ ● | major city or town |
| — | main road |
| — | main railway |
| ✈ | main airport |

The scale bar shows that every centimetre (0.4 inches) on the map is 160 kilometres (100 miles) on the ground.

---

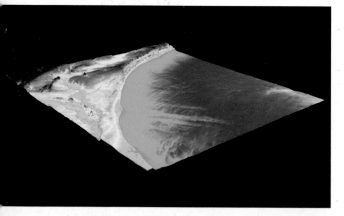

Computers can make maps that show the height of the land. The pink and blue parts are the lowest, and the orange and brown areas are the highest.

## Maps for all occasions

It is impossible to put every bit of information about a place on one map. This is why we have hundreds of types of map.

Geological maps show the types of rock found in a particular area. Mining companies use them to decide where to look for important minerals.

Weather scientists make weather maps to help forecast the weather. These maps can show in which direction a storm is moving.

28

# What is climate?

Climate is the average weather of a place over many years. The weather can change from day to day, but climate stays the same for years.

**DID YOU KNOW?**

Six thousand years ago, the Sahara Desert was covered with grass. Crocodiles and hippos lived there in rivers and lakes. Today, the Sahara Desert is the largest desert on Earth.

## Climate zones

Different parts of the world have different climates. The climate depends on how far the area is from the equator, how much rain and snow fall, and the height of the land.

The tropics have a warm climate because they are near the equator and the Sun shines overhead all year long. The Arctic and Antarctic have a cold climate because they are far from the equator and receive less sunlight over the year.

**Key**

**tropical**
- rain all year
- monsoon
- dry winters

**polar region**
- rain all year
- dry winters
- dry all year

**hot desert**
- no reliable rain
- a little rain

**temperate**
- no dry season
- dry winters

**mountain**
- weather varies with height

**mediterranean**
- warm with dry summers

This map shows the world's major climate zones.

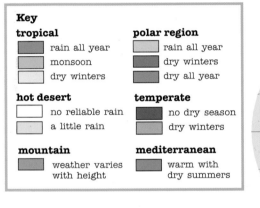

## Climate change

Climates change very slowly over thousands of years. This is a natural process. Today, humans are changing the Earth's climate. We burn coal, oil, and gas, which produces carbon dioxide gas.

Carbon dioxide in the air acts like a blanket around the Earth, keeping the Sun's heat in. The Earth is becoming warmer because of the extra carbon dioxide in the air.

Climate change could create new deserts.

## Oceans and winds

Climates are affected by ocean currents and winds. Some ocean currents bring warm water, and warm, rainy weather to an area. Others bring cold water, and cool, dry weather. Winds can bring warm air to cold places, or moist air to dry places.

# What is weather?

Weather is what is happening in the atmosphere around you.
The rain, wind, clouds, and sunshine are all part of the weather.

## Sun and wind

All weather happens because the Sun warms the Earth. Warmed air rises, and then cools and sinks back down. This movement creates winds.

Weather scientists send balloons into the atmosphere. The balloons take measurements that the scientists use to detect rainstorms.

## Clouds and rain

When the Sun heats water on the Earth's surface, the water evaporates (turns from a liquid to a gas) and rises into the air. As air rises it cools and the water vapour condenses (turns from a gas into a liquid). The water droplets form clouds. Eventually, rain may fall from the clouds.

## Air masses

An air mass is a large region of air. Air masses can be cool or warm. They can be 10 kilometres (6 miles) high and cover millions of square kilometres.

A large air mass can bring several days of dry, sunny, breezy weather. Or it can bring a few days of cloudy, rainy weather. A front is where two air masses meet. Most storms form on fronts.

When a warm air mass runs into a cold air mass, the warm, moist air rises. Clouds and rainstorms develop.

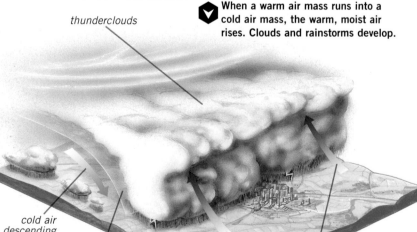

thunderclouds

cold air descending

cold front

warm air rising

# Water cycle

The journey of the Earth's water from the oceans to the atmosphere and back to the oceans again is called the water cycle.

▼ Water moves around and around in a process called the water cycle.

## Water from the oceans

When it is heated, water can change easily from a solid or liquid to a gas. Water from the Earth's oceans, seas, rivers, and lakes is heated by the Sun. It evaporates into the atmosphere. Once in the atmosphere, the water vapour is blown all around the world by the wind.

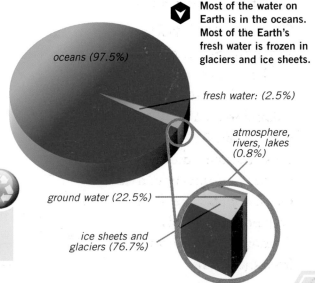

clouds
rain
snow
condensation
evaporation
evaporation
ground water
sea
lake
river

◀ On Earth, water exists as a solid (ice), a liquid (water), and a gas (water vapour in clouds).

## Clouds and rain

When air cools, the water vapour in the atmosphere condenses. It forms tiny water droplets, which make clouds. Clouds drop their water as rain, snow, or hail over the land and oceans.

## Back to the oceans

Some rain runs across the land. Trickles of water form streams, and streams join together to form rivers. Some water sinks into the ground. Eventually all the water makes its way back to the oceans. The cycle starts all over again.

▼ Most of the water on Earth is in the oceans. Most of the Earth's fresh water is frozen in glaciers and ice sheets.

oceans (97.5%)

fresh water: (2.5%)

atmosphere, rivers, lakes (0.8%)

ground water (22.5%)

ice sheets and glaciers (76.7%)

**DID YOU KNOW?**

*Water that evaporates from the ocean may return in hours, or it may fall as rain far away from the oceans and sink into rocks. It can take millions of years to return.*

# Clouds

If you looked down on the Earth from space you would see swirling white patterns. These patterns are clouds.

Clouds are made of water droplets, ice, dust, and air. Clouds form when air cools down.

## The atmosphere

The Earth is surrounded by a layer of gases – the atmosphere. The lower part of Earth's atmosphere is full of water vapour. We can't see the water in the air because water vapour is a colourless gas.

Different types of cloud have different shapes. They form at varying heights in the atmosphere.

| Key | | |
|---|---|---|
| 1 cirrus | 4 | altostratus |
| 2 cirrocumulus | 5 | cumulonimbus |
| 3 altocumulus | 6 | stratus |
| | 7 | cumulus |

This photograph was taken from space. It shows clouds in the Earth's atmosphere.

## How clouds form

Warm air can hold more water vapour than cold air. When the air cools, some of the water vapour condenses (becomes liquid). Tiny water droplets form.

If the air is cold enough, the water will form ice crystals instead of droplets. The ice crystals or water droplets group together to form clouds.

## Dust

Clouds need dust to form. In the air there is salt from the oceans, ash from volcanoes, tiny bits of soil and rock from the land, and soot from factories. This dust attracts water particles. The particles gather into droplets. Without dust, it would be difficult for clouds to form.

# Rain and snow

Rain falls when clouds can no longer hold their water droplets.
Most clouds also contain ice crystals. If it is cold enough, the crystals
may join together and fall as snow.

## How rain forms

If the water droplets in clouds are
very small and far apart, the air
holds them up. If the droplets are
close together, they start to join.
Eventually, the droplets become too
big and heavy to stay up in the
cloud. They fall as rain.

Monsoon rains are
heavy, seasonal rains.
They can cause
severe flooding.

As water droplets
fall through a
cloud they collect
more droplets.

**DID YOU KNOW?**

A falling raindrop
is made up of
about one
million droplets.

### FAST FACTS

- Sleet forms when
  raindrops partly
  freeze as they fall.
- Hail forms when
  a piece of dust
  gets covered in
  layers of ice.
- Hailstones grow
  bigger as they
  are covered in
  more ice.
- Hailstones can
  grow as big as
  golf balls.

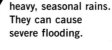

## Cooling clouds

Rain falls from clouds when the clouds
cool down. This happens when the clouds
rise higher in the atmosphere where it is
colder. More water vapour condenses into
droplets. Bigger droplets form and fall to
the ground.

## Snow

Most clouds contain ice crystals as well as
water droplets. As the air cools, the ice
crystals grow. They get so big that they fall
to the ground. If the air is less than 0°C
(32°F) all the way from the cloud to the
ground, we get snow.

# Thunder and lightning

Whenever you hear thunder, you can be sure there is lightning somewhere nearby. Lightning happens when electricity flows between thunderclouds and the ground.

Lightning bolts are huge surges of electricity.

Towering clouds mean a thunderstorm may soon happen.

## Lightning

During a thunderstorm, electricity builds up in the clouds. Electricity can move easily through materials such as metal, but it has trouble moving through air. Air usually stops electricity from flowing, in the same way as a dam stops water from flowing.

In a thunderstorm, so much electricity builds up that the 'dam' of air breaks. A bolt of electricity rushes between the clouds and the ground.

## Thunder

A lightning bolt heats the air around it. When air is heated, it expands (grows bigger). Lightning makes the air expand so quickly that it creates sound – thunder.

A storm approaching from the right. You can see the heavy rain falling.

## Time delay

Light travels very quickly. We see lightning as it happens, even if it is very far away.

Sound travels a million times more slowly. It takes thunder three seconds to travel a distance of one kilometre (0.6 miles). If a storm is a few kilometres away, we see the lightning before we hear the thunder.

To work out how far you are from a storm, count the seconds between the lightning and the thunder. Divide the answer by three to get the distance in kilometres.

# Winds

Wind is moving air. Wind can be a gentle breeze or it can be strong enough to knock you off your feet. Wind is caused by the Sun heating the air.

## How winds are created

The Sun heats the surface of the Earth and the atmosphere above it. The warmed air rises. Cold air then moves in to take the place of the warm air. These air movements create winds.

## Trade winds

Some parts of the Earth are heated more than others. The equator receives direct sunlight all year round and has a warm climate. Heated air rises and moves away from the equator to the north and south. The air cools, sinks, and travels back towards the equator. This creates the trade winds.

This map shows the major wind patterns on Earth's surface.

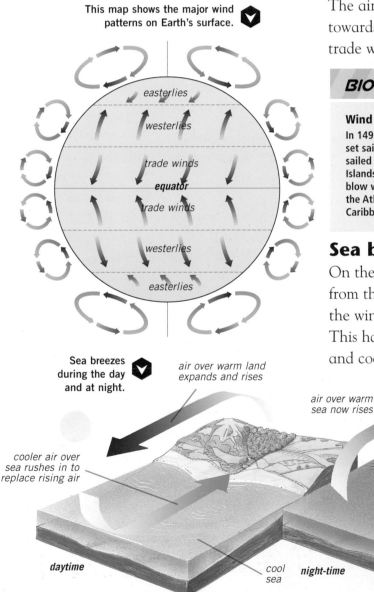

- easterlies
- westerlies
- trade winds
- equator
- trade winds
- westerlies
- easterlies

### BIOGRAPHY

**Wind and travel**
In 1492, Christopher Columbus set sail from Portugal. He sailed south to the Canary Islands. There, the trade winds blow west. He sailed across the Atlantic Ocean to the Caribbean on the trade winds.

Christopher Columbus' ship.

## Sea breezes

On the coast, a cool sea breeze blows in from the ocean during the day. At night, the winds blow from the land to the sea. This happens because the land heats up and cools down more quickly than the sea.

Sea breezes during the day and at night.

air over warm land expands and rises

air over warm sea now rises

cooler air from land rushes in to replace rising air

cooler air over sea rushes in to replace rising air

cool land

warm sea

*daytime*

*cool sea*

*night-time*

# Seasons

During the year, the seasons change. Places in the northern hemisphere (half) of the Earth have warmer weather between March and September. Places in the southern hemisphere of the Earth have warmer weather between September and March.

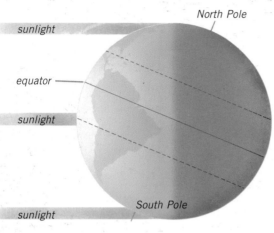

sunlight

equator

sunlight

North Pole

South Pole

sunlight

Winter is colder than summer because there is less sunlight and the Sun is lower in the sky. Less of the Sun's energy reaches the Earth's surface

## The Earth's tilt

The Earth's axis is an imaginary line between the North and the South Pole. The Earth is tilted on its axis. The Earth orbits (travels around) the Sun once each year.

- When the South Pole tilts towards the Sun it is warmer in the southern hemisphere of the Earth.

- When the North Pole tilts towards the Sun it is warmer in the northern hemisphere.

## Types of season

- Four seasons – Places that are halfway between the equator and the poles have four very different seasons: winter, spring, summer, and autumn.

- Two seasons – Near the North and South Poles there are two seasons: a light and a dark season. In summer, the Sun does not set for six months. In winter, it is dark for six months. It is cold all year long.

The Earth takes a year to make one orbit around the Sun.

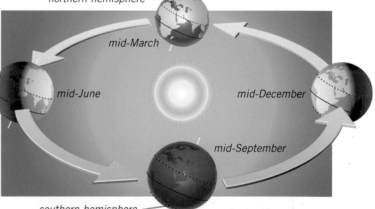

northern hemisphere

mid-March

mid-June

mid-December

mid-September

southern hemisphere

This photograph shows the position of the Sun every hour throughout the day near the North Pole in summer.

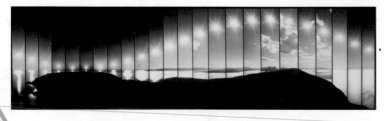

Near the equator, it is hot all year round. This is because the Sun is always high in the sky. Many regions near the equator have a rainy season in the summer and a dry season in the winter.

# Waste disposal

About 90 per cent of the world's household waste goes to landfill sites.

Newspapers, plastic bags, food scraps, cans, and bottles are all waste. After they are thrown in the bin, they are taken away. Where do they go?

## Landfill sites

A huge hole is dug in the ground and filled with rubbish. This is a landfill site. Most household rubbish is disposed (got rid) of in landfill sites.

When the hole is full, it is covered over and replanted with plants and grass. We are running out of suitable landfill sites.

## Up in smoke

Rubbish can be burnt instead of buried. The heat produced can be used for heating or making electricity. However, burning waste can create harmful gases.

**DID YOU KNOW?**

*Every day, the people of New York City, USA, throw away up to 25,000 tonnes (27,500 tons) of waste.*

## In the sewers

Sewage includes body waste from toilets, and water from sinks, washing machines, and baths. Pipes carry the sewage to treatment plants. Solids and harmful substances are removed. The water can be returned to the environment.

## Recycling

Waste paper, metals, glass, and plastic can be recycled. The different materials are processed and used again. Recycling is better for the environment than landfill sites or burning rubbish.

How a sewage treatment plant works.

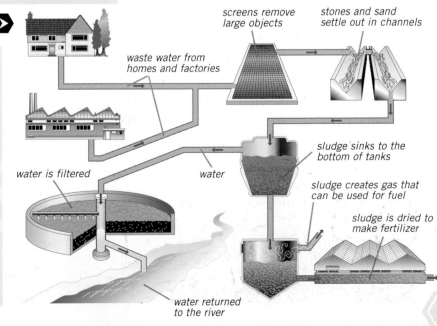

waste water from homes and factories

screens remove large objects

stones and sand settle out in channels

water is filtered

water

sludge sinks to the bottom of tanks

sludge creates gas that can be used for fuel

sludge is dried to make fertilizer

water returned to the river

# Pollution

Humans cause pollution when they damage their surroundings. Pollution includes litter, sewage, and other waste. It can damage the land, sea, and air.

## Water pollution

Sewage is liquid waste from homes and factories. If sewage gets into rivers, lakes, and oceans, it damages the environment and the plants and animals that live there.

Oil tankers carry oil across the oceans. If a tanker crashes into a rock or another ship, the oil can pour out and pollute the sea water. Thousands of sea creatures can be poisoned or killed.

## Air pollution

Car engines and factories burn fuel and give off fumes. The fumes may cause breathing problems in some people. The fumes can also mix with water in the air and form acid rain. Acid rain pollutes rivers and lakes, and can kill fish and other wildlife.

Smog is a mixture of smoke and fog or chemical fumes. It pollutes many of the world's big cities.

## The ozone layer

Ozone gas surrounds the Earth. It protects the Earth from harmful rays in sunlight. Pollution is destroying the ozone layer. Countries around the world are reducing this pollution. Nature can repair the ozone layer.

### DID YOU KNOW?

The world's worst chemical disaster happened in India in 1984. A chemical explosion released deadly gas into the air. The gas killed 3,000 people.

Burning fuel also produces carbon dioxide gas. The carbon dioxide builds up in the Earth's atmosphere. It traps the Sun's heat and is causing world temperatures to rise – global warming.

The environment is polluted in many ways.

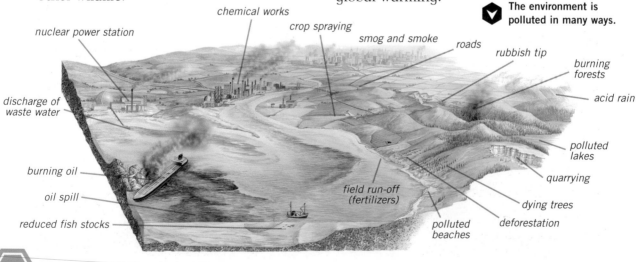

nuclear power station
chemical works
crop spraying
smog and smoke
roads
rubbish tip
burning forests
acid rain
discharge of waste water
polluted lakes
burning oil
quarrying
oil spill
field run-off (fertilizers)
dying trees
reduced fish stocks
deforestation
polluted beaches

# Global warming

The Earth is getting warmer. Scientists call this global warming, and they think that it is caused by humans polluting the air.

## The greenhouse effect

The Sun warms the Earth. Carbon dioxide, water vapour, and other gases in the atmosphere act like a blanket around the Earth. They are called greenhouse gases. They stop some of the Sun's warmth from escaping back into space. This is the natural greenhouse effect.

## Global warming

Humans burn fossil fuels – coal, oil, and gas. This pollutes the atmosphere with extra greenhouse gases. The gases build up and trap more and more heat. This is global warming.

## Climate change

If global warming continues, the Earth's climates will change. In some places, there will be more rain and flooding. Other places will turn into deserts.

Ice at the Poles will melt. The extra water will cause sea levels to rise and low-lying areas to flood. Plants and animals may not be able to cope with the new climates, and die out.

Global warming is causing glaciers and ice sheets to melt.

## Stopping global warming

To slow down global warming, we need to use less electricity, recycle rubbish, and walk or cycle instead of driving. We also need to use alternative energy sources, such as solar and wind energy.

Many different things contribute to greenhouse gases.

sunlight

some heat escapes

greenhouse gases

heat

greenhouse gases trap heat

forest fire

exhaust fumes

pollution from factories

# Recycling

Aluminium is a metal that can be recycled (used again). Glass, paper, and plastics can also be recycled.

Drinks cans are made of aluminium. The metal has probably been used before. It could have been cooking foil, milk-bottle tops, or even part of an aircraft wing.

## Why recycle?

Humans throw away lots of rubbish – waste. Recycling rubbish into new products reduces waste. Recycling also saves energy and money. It takes a lot of electricity to get aluminium out of rock. Re-melting aluminium waste uses much less energy and money.

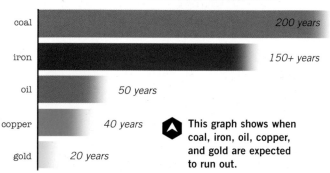

coal — 200 years
iron — 150+ years
oil — 50 years
copper — 40 years
gold — 20 years

This graph shows when coal, iron, oil, copper, and gold are expected to run out.

## Rotting away

Nature recycles many materials. Worms, insects, fungi, and bacteria can change some waste into chemicals that improve soil. New plants can be grown in the soil.

These plastic bottles are waiting to be recycled.

Everyone can get involved with recycling.

## Gone for ever

Recycling saves the Earth's resources. Paper is made from wood pulp, which comes from trees. Recycling paper means cutting down fewer trees.

Trees are a renewable resource – we can keep growing them. Other materials cannot be replaced. Plastics are made from oil, which will run out in your lifetime. This is why we need to recycle plastics.

# Renewable resources

Renewable resources can be replaced. Sunlight and the wind are renewable energy resources. They will not run out.

We use energy for cooking, heating, and powering machines. At present, fossil fuels (coal, oil, and gas) provide most of this energy. Fossil fuels cannot be replaced when they run out. They are non-renewable.

A group of wind turbines is called a wind farm.

This car is covered with solar cells. The cells use sunlight to make electricity and power the car.

## Energy crisis

Oil and gas are expected to run out by 2050. Few nuclear power stations are being built because many people think they are dangerous. Coal will only last 200 years more.

By using more renewable energy resources, fossil fuels will last longer. Also, renewable energy does not cause pollution and global warming.

## Renewable resource types

1. Wind energy – The energy of moving air turns wind turbines. They drive electricity generators.

2. Solar energy – Energy from the Sun can be trapped to create electricity.

3. Geothermal energy – In some places, hot underground rocks are near the Earth's surface. Water for homes is heated by piping it through the hot rocks.

4. Flowing water – Hydroelectric power stations use flowing water to turn turbines. The turbines drive electricity generators.

5. Wave energy – Water rises and falls in waves. Wave machines use this energy and convert it into electricity.

A waterwheel turns as water flows over the blades. Turbines in hydroelectric power stations work in a similar way.

# Conservation

Humans need land for farms, mines, and towns. We chop down forests for timber and to create fields for cattle to graze. These actions destroy the natural habitats (homes) of plants and animals. Conservation is the protection of the plants, animals, and natural habitats of our world.

This bird is covered in oil from a leaking tanker. Conservationists help animals affected by pollution.

## Let's help

Each one of us can be a conservationist. We can recycle waste. We can reduce pollution by walking or cycling instead of travelling by car.

We can join local groups that help to clean up the environment. All of us can help to raise money for worldwide conservation work.

## Governments and conservation

Governments can ban the hunting and collection of rare species (types) of plants and animals, and the sale of animals' body parts. They can set up nature reserves to protect natural habitats. Goverments can also make laws to reduce pollution. Pollution is a big threat to wildlife.

## Captivity

Rare animals can be bred in zoos. Rare plants can be grown in botanical gardens. This helps to stop species from becoming extinct (dying out).

We must preserve the habitats of wild animals and plants if they are to survive.

Golden tamarins are endangered, which means there are few of them left. Their rainforest homes are being destroyed.

Tigers, gorillas, pandas, and thousands of other animal species are in danger of extinction.

# Humans

There are more than 6.6 billion humans on Earth. Each of us has a body made up of the same basic parts, but no two humans are exactly alike.

Scientists have found fossils (preserved remains) of ancient humans from millions of years ago. The scientific name for modern humans (us) is *Homo sapiens.*

Early humans drew pictures of their surroundings. These engravings were made around 10,000 years ago.

## Ancient human remains

In 1974, the remains of an ancient human were found in Ethiopia, Africa. The skeleton is thought to be three million years old. Scientists think that the skeleton is female so they called her Lucy. Her teeth, jaws, and many other features are similar to a modern human.

## Early humans

Around 100,000 years ago, humans got their food from wild plants and animals. It wasn't until about 10,000 years ago that people started to farm. They planted crops. They tamed and kept animals. Many settled in villages. Over time, the villages grew into the towns and cities that we know today.

## What is a human?

Two features make humans special.

1. Humans have long thumbs. This makes it possible for us to carry out delicate tasks such as writing and sewing.

2. Humans have large brains. We are probably the most intelligent animal that has ever lived on Earth. Our intelligence has allowed us to make tools, build homes, travel, and to develop language.

Thousands of years ago, humans used cave paintings and carvings to communicate with each other.

**DID YOU KNOW?**

*In prehistoric times, people lived to an average age of 18 years. Today, people in the developed world live to an average age of 76 years.*

## Cells

A human body is made of millions of tiny building blocks called cells. Each human body is made of about 50 million million cells.

## Growth and repair

When we grow, we produce more cells. If we are injured and our cells are damaged, they must be replaced. Most cells can divide in two to create new cells.

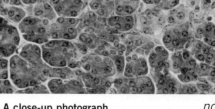

A close-up photograph of human cells.

The organs of the human body. The organs work together and form body systems.

*brain, spinal cord, and nerves control the body and carry information*

*nose, windpipe, and lungs take in oxygen from the air*

*mouth, stomach, and intestines digest food*

*heart, blood vessels, and blood carry oxygen around the body*

*kidneys and bladder take waste from the blood out of the body in the urine*

**DID YOU KNOW?**

*It would take 100,000 cells to cover a pinhead.*

*bones and muscles keep us upright and allow us to move*

## Tissues and organs

Groups of similar cells work together. These groups are called tissues. For example, muscle cells form muscle tissue.

Different tissues group together to form organs. The heart is an organ.

It contains muscle and nerve tissue. Some groups of organs work together. The digestive system is a group of organs that help us digest (take the goodness from) food.

# Skin and hair

Skin covers your entire body. It is made of skin cells. It is strong and waterproof, but it is also soft and stretchy.

Hair and nails grow from your skin. They are made of dead cells.

## Protection

Skin is a few millimetres thick. It creates a barrier against the outside world. As long as it is not cut or scratched, it can keep out germs.

New skin cells are produced all the time. They replace skin that wears away, and they repair cuts.

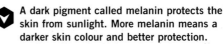 A dark pigment called melanin protects the skin from sunlight. More melanin means a darker skin colour and better protection.

The skin on your fingertips and lips are the most sensitive parts of your body. ❯

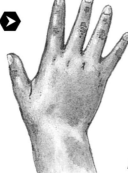

**DID YOU KNOW?**

*Every person on Earth has a different fingerprint – the swirling patterns of ridges on our fingertips.*

## Nails and hair

Both nails and hair are made of dead cells that are hardened by a substance called keratin. We only have long hair on our heads. The rest of the body has short hair. Each hair has its own tiny muscle to lift it when we are cold.

## Temperature control

The temperature inside our bodies is 37°C (98.6°F). Skin helps us to keep this temperature steady.

In hot weather, sweat glands in the skin produce sweat to cool us down. In cold weather, blood vessels in the skin shut down to keep the warm blood away from the cold air.

A cross-section through the skin. ⬇

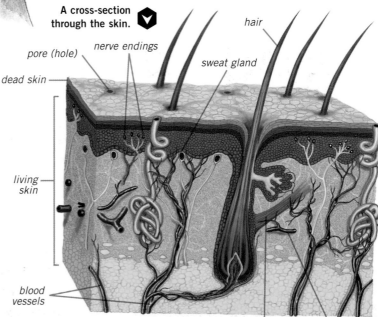

pore (hole)

nerve endings

hair

sweat gland

dead skin

living skin

blood vessels

muscle

oil gland

# Ears

Your sense of hearing helps you understand what is going on in the world around you.

Your ears collect sounds and send the information to your brain. Your brain makes sense of the sound information.

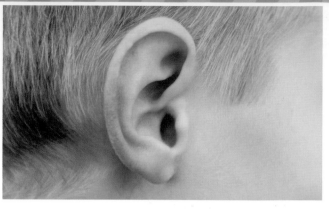

A human ear guides sound into the ear, towards the eardrum.

## Human ears

Human ears have a funnel shape. The funnel collects sound waves. Next, the sound waves hit the eardrum, which is a thin membrane (skin). The sound waves make the eardrum vibrate (wobble). The vibrations pass through a set of tiny bones. The bones make the sound louder and pass it on to the inner ear, which is full of liquid. The liquid moves tiny hairs inside the inner ear, which help to send electrical messages to the brain.

## Other ears

Mammals such as foxes have huge ears. Large ears can pick up sounds too quiet for humans to hear. Bats are mammals that mostly hunt in the dark. Bats make bursts of short, high-pitched sounds. They listen for the echoes to come back. The pattern of echoes tells them about their surroundings.

A bat's ears can detect sounds that are too high for us to hear.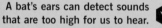

## Hearing

Hearing is very important in the natural world. Animals such as rabbits need to know if there is any danger nearby. Their ears turn and twitch as they feed, listening for the tiniest sounds. If they hear a fox approaching, they turn and run to their burrows.

**DID YOU KNOW?**

Many insects hear with their legs. Some hear with the sides of their bodies.

A rabbit's ears act as an early-warning system. They can detect very quiet sounds. This helps the rabbit to keep away from dangerous animals.

# Eyes

We get 80 per cent of our information about the world around us through our eyes. For animals such as birds of prey, sight is even more important. Nearly all animals have eyes of some sort.

## The human eye

Light bounces off everything around you. It enters the eye through the pupil. The pupil is the black hole in the centre of the iris (the coloured part of your eye).

The iris can change the size of the pupil. When it is dark it makes the pupil bigger, so that more light can enter. In bright sunlight, the pupil becomes smaller.

## Sight problems

If light doesn't fall directly on the retina, the person may have a problem seeing clearly. This can usually be corrected by wearing glasses. Glasses contain lenses that bend the light to make sure it falls directly on the retina.

The light travels through the lens, which is a clear disc. The lens bends the light to focus the image, like the lens in a camera. The light hits the back of the eye – the retina. It forms an image on the retina, but the image is upside down. The brain turns it the right way up.

The parts of the human eye. ▼

lens

pupil

iris

nerve to the brain

retina

## Other eyes

Animals' eyes often provide good clues about how they live. Owls, cats, and other creatures that are mostly active at night have very large pupils. This means that they can gather in as much light as possible.

 A fly's eye contains many lenses. The fly's brain puts together images from each lens to see an image of its surroundings.

# Heart and blood

Your heart beats non-stop, 24 hours a day, 7 days a week. If you live to be 70 years old, that comes to more than 2.5 billion heartbeats!

The heart pumps blood around the body through tubes called blood vessels.

## Blood vessels

Arteries are the largest and strongest blood vessels. They carry blood that contains oxygen gas away from the heart. When the oxygen has been used up by the body, veins carry the blood back to the heart.

Blood cells magnified 1,200 times. The blue and green circles are white blood cells. The red discs are red blood cells.

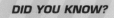

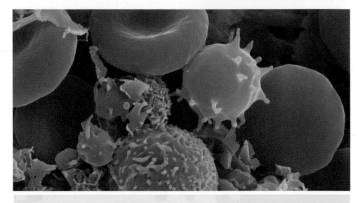

## What is blood?

Human blood contains different types of cell. Red blood cells pick up oxygen in the lungs. White blood cells fight infection. All the blood cells are swept along in a liquid called plasma.

Blood must supply the body with oxygen.

## The heart

The right side of the heart receives blood from the body and sends it to the lungs. In the lungs, the blood picks up oxygen. The blood returns to the left side of the heart.

The left side of the heart pumps the blood to the organs and muscles all over the body.

Blood travels from the right side of the heart to the lungs and back to the heart. Then it travels away from the left side of the heart and around the rest of the body.

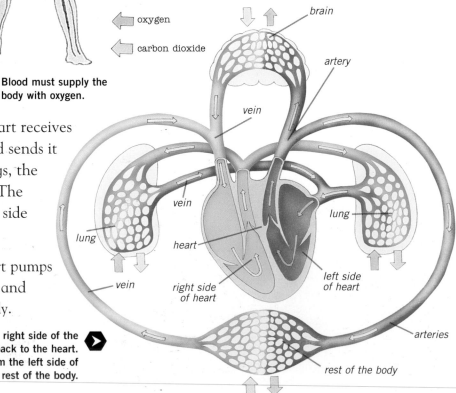

oxygen

carbon dioxide

brain

artery

vein

vein

lung

lung

left side of heart

vein

right side of heart

heart

arteries

rest of the body

# Lungs and breathing

You breathe every few seconds. You may take as many as 20,000 breaths every day!

Humans need oxygen gas, which is present in the air. During breathing, the lungs take oxygen from the air.

## In and out

Your nose, windpipe, lungs, and chest muscles make up your breathing system. When you breathe in, your lungs fill with air. Oxygen enters your blood and then travels around your body, giving you energy.

When you breathe out, you push waste gases out of your lungs. Carbon dioxide is a waste gas.

air in

When you breathe in, a muscle called the diaphragm moves down. Air is pulled into the lungs.

air out

ribs out

ribs in

diaphragm down

diaphragm up

When you breathe out, the diaphragm moves up. Air is pushed out of the lungs.

## Inside the lungs

The lungs contain lots of branching passageways. Each tiny passageway ends in a group of air sacs called alveoli. There are hundreds of millions of aveoli in your lungs.

Oxygen moves from the alveoli into your blood. Carbon dioxide moves from your blood into the alveoli.

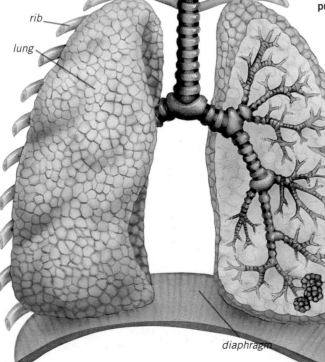

windpipe

rib

lung

alveoli

diaphragm

 The alveoli are arranged in groups that look a bit like bunches of grapes.

**DID YOU KNOW?**

If all your aveoli were laid out flat, they would cover a tennis court.

# Bones and muscles

Your skeleton has more than 200 living bones. It supports you and keeps you upright.

Your muscles are attached to your skeleton. They pull on your bones to make you move.

The longest bones contain bone marrow. Bone marrow makes red blood cells.

Some of the bones and joints of the skeleton.

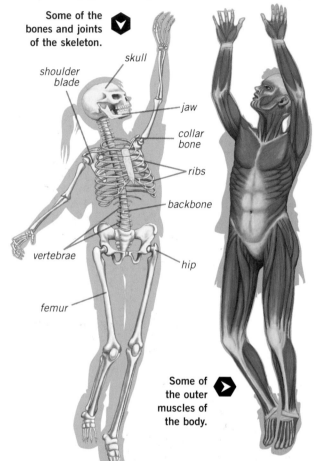

- skull
- shoulder blade
- jaw
- collar bone
- ribs
- backbone
- vertebrae
- hip
- femur

Some of the outer muscles of the body.

## Bony protection

Bones are hard, strong, and light. Without bones our bodies would be soft and floppy.

**DID YOU KNOW?**

Your smallest bone is in your ear. It is about the size of one grain of rice.

Most organs of the body are soft and delicate. Bones protect these soft organs. The skull bones form a case around the brain. The ribs form a cage around the lungs and heart.

## Joints

Bones meet each other at joints. We have different types of joint for moving in different ways.

Hinge joints at the knee and elbow allow our limbs to bend in one direction. Ball-and-socket joints at the shoulder and hip allow movement in almost any direction.

## Muscles and movement

A human has about 600 muscles. They allow us to control how we move. Muscles attach to two bones across a joint. We tell our muscles when to contract (shorten). The contraction pulls the bones and makes them move.

Muscles work in pairs. One muscle contracts to move a joint in one direction. Its partner contracts to move the joint back again.

- biceps contracts
- arm bends
- arm straightens
- triceps contracts

# Digestion

When you eat, you start your food on a 9-metre (30-foot) journey through your body. The journey may take more than a day.

Your body will digest (take the goodness from) the food and get rid of the waste.

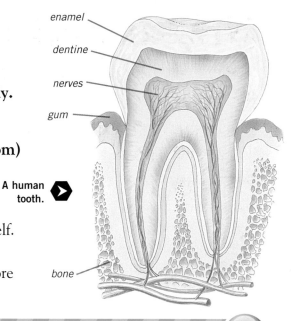

A human tooth. ▶

- enamel
- dentine
- nerves
- gum
- bone

## Why do we need food?

Food helps the body to work, grow, and repair itself. It contains the nutrients we need for good health. Food must be broken down into smaller parts before the body can use it.

Humans must eat a healthy, balanced diet to stay strong and well. ▲

## Mouth to the stomach

In the mouth, teeth tear and grind food into tiny pieces. The food travels down the food pipe to the stomach. It stays in the stomach for about three hours. Here, juices break down the food.

## Stomach to the rectum

The broken down food travels along the small intestine. Nutrients move out of the intestine and into the blood.

Undigested food passes into the large intestine. The food is stored in the rectum until it leaves the body through the anus.

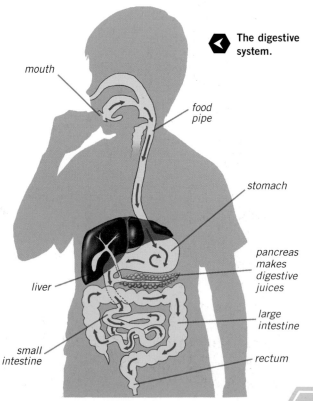

◀ The digestive system.

- mouth
- food pipe
- stomach
- liver
- pancreas makes digestive juices
- large intestine
- small intestine
- rectum

# Brain and nerves

The brain is the body's control centre. Nerves reach out from the brain, down the spinal cord, and to the rest of the body.

The brain, spinal cord, and nerves together make up the nervous system.

> Nerves connect your brain to every part of your body.

## Nerve cells

Nerve cells are called neurons. There are billions of connected neurons in the brain. Neurons branch off the spinal cord to the rest of the body.

Electrical pulses shoot along the neurons. The pulses carry instructions from the brain to the rest of the body, and carry information about the outside world to the brain.

## The brain

Different parts of the brain carry out different jobs. The main part of the brain is the cerebrum. It controls speech and the senses, and it does all of the thinking. It lets us create memories and learn.

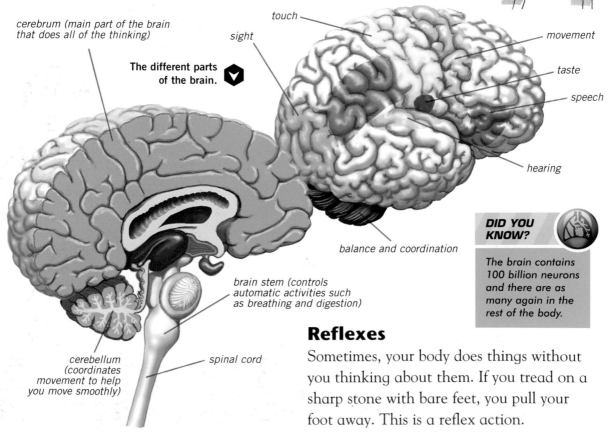

cerebrum (main part of the brain that does all of the thinking)

sight

touch

movement

taste

speech

hearing

**The different parts of the brain.**

balance and coordination

brain stem (controls automatic activities such as breathing and digestion)

cerebellum (coordinates movement to help you move smoothly)

spinal cord

## Reflexes

Sometimes, your body does things without you thinking about them. If you tread on a sharp stone with bare feet, you pull your foot away. This is a reflex action.

## Learning and remembering

Your brain contains more than 100 billion nerve cells. Each nerve cell is connected to thousands of others. As you learn new skills, the nerve cells make new connections.

We learn by trial and error. Babies pick up a rattle and discover that shaking it makes a noise.

We learn from experience. We remember which key opens a door – we do not have to try each key in the bunch every time. We also learn by copying others.

▲ Emotions can be shared by large groups of people. You can see by their faces that these people are happy.

### Memory game

Imagine you need to remember to buy six things. Think of a story that links these things. The story will help you to remember the list.

1. You are eating sausages but they are covered with stamps.
2. You wash the stamps off the sausages with shampoo.
3. The sausages turn into chocolate. You eat the chocolate and read a comic.
4. A birthday card falls out of the comic.

Shopping list
sausages
postage stamps
shampoo
chocolate
a comic
a birthday card

## Emotions

Emotions are strong feelings such as love, hate, and anger. These feelings begin in the brain but can affect the whole body. If we are sad or very happy, we may burst into tears.

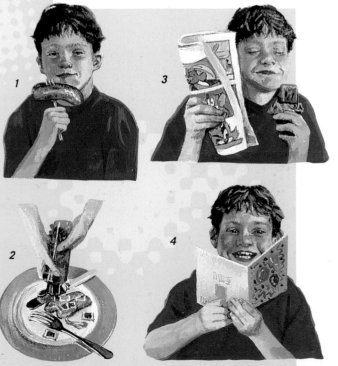

# Human senses

Your senses tell you what is going on in the world around you.

Your sense organs are your eyes, ears, skin, tongue, and nose. They collect information and send it along nerves to your brain. Your brain turns the information into sights, sounds, touches, tastes, and smells.

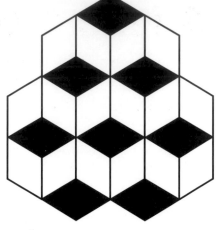

Our eyes can be fooled. How many cubes can you see in this picture? Depending on how you look at it, you might count six or seven.

## BIOGRAPHY

**Louis Braille**
Blind people can use their sense of touch to read a type of writing called Braille. The letters are patterns of dots raised from the paper. Braille is named after its inventor, the Frenchman Louis Braille (1809–1852).

This child is running his fingers across the bumps to read Braille.

## FAST FACTS

Humans can detect the following basic tastes:
- ☐ Sweet
- ☐ Sour
- ☐ Bitter
- ☐ Salt
- ☐ Umami (a savoury, meaty taste)

## Sight

Each of our eyes detects light. Nerves send information about the light to the brain. The brain uses the information from each eye to put together a three-dimensional picture of the surroundings.

## Hearing

Sounds make the insides of our ears vibrate (wobble backwards and forwards). The vibrations make thousands of tiny hairs move. The hairs are connected to nerves. The nerves pass the sound information to the brain.

Our sense organs for sight, smell, and taste are on the front of the head.

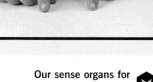

smell detectors

eye (sight)

nose (smell)

tongue (taste)

### DID YOU KNOW?

*Taste and smell are linked. When we have a blocked nose and can't smell, our food does not taste as good.*

# Speech and language

Speech is a type of communication. You learn to speak in the first few years of life. You learn the language spoken by the people around you when you are very young.

**DID YOU KNOW?**

There are more than 6,500 languages spoken in the world.

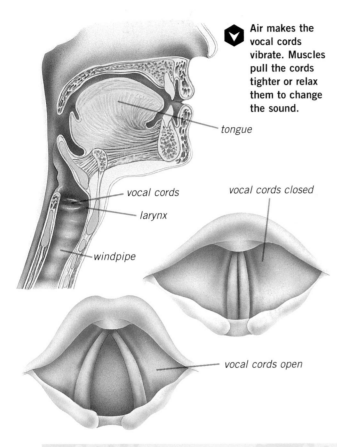

Air makes the vocal cords vibrate. Muscles pull the cords tighter or relax them to change the sound.

tongue

vocal cords

larynx

windpipe

vocal cords closed

vocal cords open

## First words

Babies babble and make funny sounds. As they grow older, they copy what they hear and put words together.

By the age of three, most children know how to speak in sentences. As we grow and develop, we learn to use language to communicate ideas and feelings.

## How do we speak?

We have vocal cords in our windpipe. When we breathe, air passes over them. If we tighten our vocal cords, they vibrate (wobble backwards and forwards) when air passes over them. This makes sounds.

When we speak, we tighten and relax our vocal cords very fast. We change the shape of our mouth, and move our tongue, lips, and teeth. This creates speech.

## Body language

We can communicate with our hands and bodies. You can see when someone is angry by looking at their face. Nodding or shaking the head can take the place of words.

People who are deaf can communicate using their hands and faces. This is called sign language.

This person is using sign language to say 'Hello! I am pleased to meet you.'

Hello!    I (am)    pleased    to meet    you.

# Health

It is important to look after your body so that you stay healthy. Diet, exercise, and the place that you live all affect your health.

People live longer when their water is clean and they have good medical care.

## Water

People need a clean water supply to stay healthy. Dirty water can spread diseases. In some countries, people die each year from a disease called malaria. Malaria is carried by mosquitoes. The mosquitoes breed in dirty water.

## Diet and exercise

A healthy diet and regular exercise are important for good health. A healthy diet contains foods for energy and plenty of vitamins. You need vitamins to help fight infection.

Regular exercise improves your heart and lungs, and makes your muscles stronger.

These people in West Africa are being given a pill to prevent a disease called river blindness.

## Vaccinations

Vaccinations help prevent disease and keep people healthy. Vaccination programmes have got rid of a disease called smallpox. They have also reduced deaths from polio and saved thousands of lives.

Regular exercise keeps the heart and other muscles fit and healthy.

# Diet

Food gives us energy to keep us alive and healthy. Food contains the nutrients (goodness) that our bodies need to build everything – from muscles and bones to the brain and the heart.

## A balanced diet

Eating a balanced diet means getting a good mixture of all the food types. There are three main food groups – carbohydrates, proteins, and fats. We also need other nutrients called vitamins and minerals.

fatty and sugary foods

protein foods

fruit and vegetables

carbohydrates

The foods that make up a healthy diet. You should eat more of the foods at the bottom of the pyramid and less of the foods at the top.

wheat
rice
potato
cassava
soya bean
sorghum

Wheat and potatoes are grown in cooler parts of the world. Millet, rice, sorghum, soya, and cassava are grown in Africa and Asia. These foods contain carbohydrates.

## Energy and growth

Carbohydrates, such as pasta, bread, and rice, give us energy. We need protein so that our bodies grow and repair themselves. Protein is found in meat, fish, cheese, and beans.

Fats also give us energy, but too much fat can be bad for us. It can damage the heart.

**FAST FACTS**

A balanced diet is a mixture of:
☐ Carbohydrates – bread, pasta, potatoes
☐ Vitamins and minerals – fruit, vegetables
☐ Protein – meat, fish, cheese
☐ Fats – butter, oil

This healthy meal contains carbohydrates, proteins, and fats.

## Vitamins and minerals

Fruits and vegetables contain vitamins and minerals. They help to keep our bodies working properly and help to protect us from illness.

Vitamin C is found in oranges, and vitamin A is found in carrots. Milk contains a mineral called calcium, which we need for healthy bones.

# Growth and development

Babies grow to become children and then adults. The shape of their bodies change. Their minds develop. They become able to do all sorts of things such as running, reading, and writing.

Reading is a good way to learn about the world.

## Babies and children

Childhood is when most growing and learning happens. Babies are almost helpless, but their bodies and minds develop quickly. They become stronger and better able to control their movements.

Within one or two years they begin to walk and talk. By the age of five they can speak well, draw, and may start to read.

young adult

You can see how boys' and girls' bodies change as they grow up.

child

baby

young adult

child

adolescent
(at puberty)

toddler

baby

toddler

adolescent (at puberty)

## Growing older

When you are an adult, your body stops growing, but it still changes. Around the age of 20, your muscles and brain are in peak condition.

As people become old, their skin wrinkles, and their eyes and ears do not work as well. Eventually, people's bodies wear out and they die.

It is important to keep your mind and body fit and healthy whatever your age.

## Childhood to adulthood

During childhood you continue to grow. Puberty is when you change from a child to an adult. This begins in your early teens and lasts until you are between 16 and 20 years old. Your body changes and develops. The changes make it possible for you to have your own children one day.

# Diseases

Some diseases, such as the common cold, cause us no lasting harm. Colds are spread by a germ called a virus.

Other diseases, such as heart disease, are very serious. They can often be controlled by medicines. Heart disease cannot be spread.

## Infectious diseases

Diseases that can be caught are called infectious diseases. Bacteria and viruses are germs that can make us ill. They are spread through the air, water, or food, or by other animals.

If germs enter our bodies, we can catch a disease. Influenza is an infectious disease caused by a virus. It is spread through the air when an infected person coughs or sneezes.

Millions of bacteria and viruses fly out every time we sneeze.

## Non-infectious diseases

Other diseases, such as heart disease, are not caught from other people. They can be caused by the way we live and the food we eat.

Some diseases, such as cancer, can be passed down by our parents or caused by chemicals in the environment. Scientists do not know the causes of all diseases.

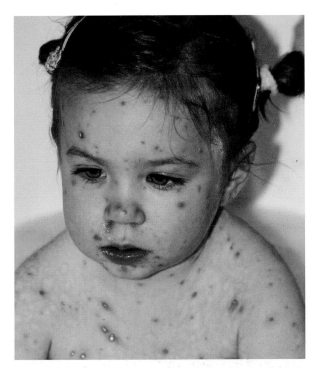

This child is infected with the chicken pox virus.

**BIOGRAPHY**

**Louis Pasteur**
Louis Pasteur (1822–1895) was a French chemist. He was the first person to realize that diseases are caused by germs. He found a vaccine for anthrax, a deadly disease of animals.

# Cancers

Cancer is not a single disease. Different cancers can affect different parts of the body.

Doctors do not always know why some people get cancer and others don't. Many cancers can be treated with powerful medicines.

## Cancer cells

Our bodies are made of millions of cells. The cells divide to create new cells, which replace old ones.

Sometimes the process goes wrong, and a cancer cell forms. Cancer cells divide very quickly and form lumps called tumours. Tumours can stop the body from working properly.

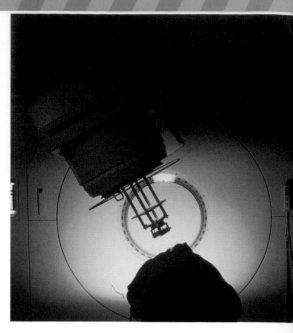

Radiotherapy is one treatment of cancer. Radiation is used to kill cancer cells.

## Cancer causes

Some cancers are caused by faulty genes. Genes are the instructions that make you who you are. They are found in your cells. Other cancers are caused by chemicals in the environment, or by germs.

## Cancer treatment

Most cancers can be treated successfully if they are caught early. An operation can sometimes take out the tumour. The patient may be given strong drugs to kill any cancer cells that are left. This is called chemotherapy.

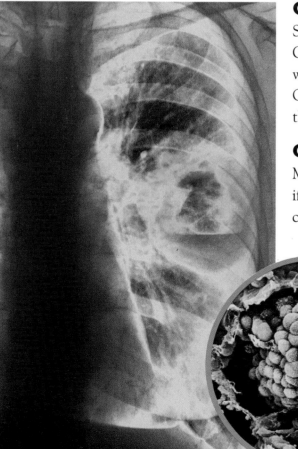

This X-ray shows a tumour in the lungs. The inset shows a close-up of the tumour.

# Medicine

You may have visited a doctor when you were unwell. Doctors know a lot about how the body works and what causes illness. They prescribe medicines to cure diseases or to reduce symptoms.

**DID YOU KNOW?**

In the past, one of the most popular cures for illness was applying leeches to suck blood from the patient.

## Diagnosis

Doctors use simple ways to diagnose (find out) what is wrong. They look inside the mouth for signs of infection. Stethoscopes let them listen to heart and lung sounds.

Doctors take samples of urine and blood and send them for testing. These tests look for germs and other substances, which help to diagnose the illness.

 **FAST FACTS**

**Health workers**

- ☐ Nurses – Care for people with all types of illness.
- ☐ Physiotherapists – Treat breathing problems, muscle stiffness, pain, and injury.
- ☐ Chiropodists – Treat foot problems.
- ☐ Surgeons – Carry out operations.
- ☐ Radiographers – Take X-rays.

A doctor may listen to a patient's heart when diagnosing an illness.

## Medicines and cures

Modern drugs are made in large factories, but many were first discovered in natural substances. Aspirin came from the bark of a willow tree.

One of the most important medicines are antibiotics, which kill bacteria (a type of germ).

## Technology

Advances in technology help doctors treat very ill people. Patients who are seriously ill may go into an intensive care unit. Machines do their breathing for them. Tubes deliver drugs straight into their blood. Other machines constantly check on the patients' heartbeat.

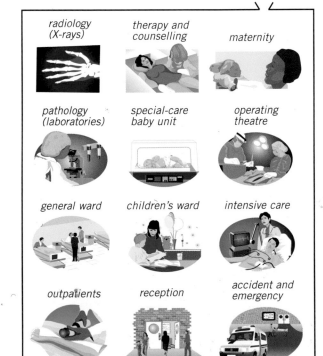

radiology (X-rays)

therapy and counselling

maternity

pathology (laboratories)

special-care baby unit

operating theatre

general ward

children's ward

intensive care

outpatients

reception

accident and emergency

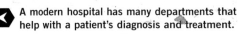

A modern hospital has many departments that help with a patient's diagnosis and treatment.

# Cells

What do you have in common with a tree, a worm, and a crocodile? The answer is cells. All living things are made up of tiny building blocks called cells.

Very simple living things are made of just one cell. A tiny worm has about 1,000 cells and an adult human being has about ten million million cells.

## What are cells?

Cells are tiny. They can only be seen with a microscope. A microscope makes things look bigger. Cells are like tiny factories. Inside cells, energy is released from food to give you energy. You use the energy to breathe, move, and carry out all of your everyday activities.

**BIOGRAPHY**

**Robert Hooke**
Robert Hooke (1635–1703) built his own microscope. He looked at cells from cork trees under the microscope. He was the first person to draw pictures of cells viewed in this way.

This is what Robert ▶ Hooke's microscope looked like.

## Cell contents

Each cell is a bag full of jelly-like fluid called cytoplasm. The control centre of a cell is called the nucleus. Genes are found inside the nucleus. They are the instructions that make you who you are. Each gene is a section of a long strand of DNA.

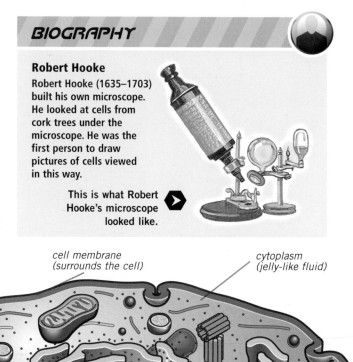

cell membrane (surrounds the cell)

cytoplasm (jelly-like fluid)

nucleus (contains genes)

mitochondria (produce energy)

An animal cell is about ▶ 0.02 millimetres (0.0008 inches) across.

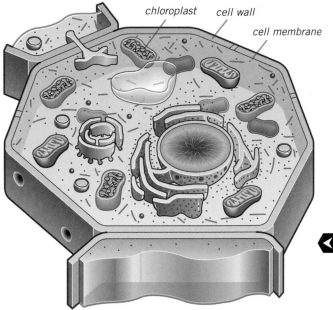

chloroplast    cell wall

cell membrane

## Plant and animal cells

There are differences between plant and animal cells. Plant cells have a thick cell wall. Animal cells do not have a cell wall.

Plant cells contain chloroplasts. Plants use the chloroplasts to make their own food. Animal cells do not have chloroplasts.

◄ A typical plant cell is enclosed by a thick cell wall outside the cell membrane. Plant cells contain chloroplasts for making food.

## Simple cells

Bacteria are tiny living things. Some bacteria cause disease but many are helpful. You have helpful bacteria inside you to help you digest (take the goodness from) food. Bacteria have much smaller, simpler cells than other living things. They have no nucleus.

Bacteria are usually made of one simple cell. This bacterium is dividing ► in two to create a new bacterium.

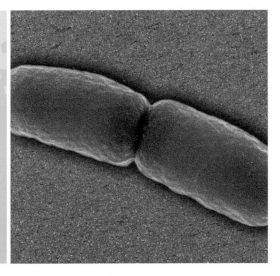

## Working together

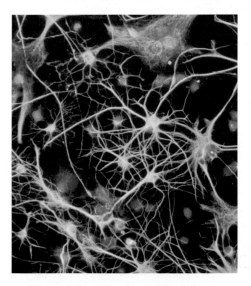

In large living things, there are many different types of cell. A rabbit has more than 250 different types of cell. You have about 200 different types of cell.

Groups of similar cells are packed together to form tissues. Lots of nerve cells are packed together to make nerve tissue. In most plants and animals, separate tissues are joined together to form organs. Leaves, flowers, lungs, and eyes are organs.

◄ A microscope picture of lots of nerve cells connected together. Long, thin nerve strands branch off from the circular, central parts of the nerve cells.

# Classification

Classification is a way of organizing all the living things on Earth. Scientists group together living things that share certain features.

## Tiger classification

The scientific naming system was invented by a Swedish naturalist called Linnaeus in the 18th century. In his system, each group is divided into smaller groups. This table shows how a tiger is classified.

| Group | Subdivision | Meaning |
|---|---|---|
| Kingdom | Animals | |
| Phylum | Chordata | Nerve cord down back |
| Sub-phylum | Vertebrates | Having a backbone |
| Class | Mammals | Animal with fur or hair, feeds on mother's milk |
| Order | Carnivores | Meat-eating |
| Family | Felidae | Cats |
| Genus | Panthera | Big cats |
| Species | Panthera tigris | Tiger |

A tiger's two-part name tells us that it is a tiger (*tigris*) that belongs to the big cat group (*Panthera*).

## Kingdoms to species

Scientists usually split living things into five kingdoms – animals, plants, fungi, protists, and monerans.

Each kingdom contains thousands of different species of living things. Gorillas are one species, and human beings are another species. A male and female of the same species can breed together.

## How are living things classified?

Scientists classify living things by their shape, appearance, and the way they develop. Scientists also compare DNA and genes to help classify living things.

Today, the living world is usually divided into five kingdoms. The number beneath the name of each kingdom is the number of species found in that kingdom.

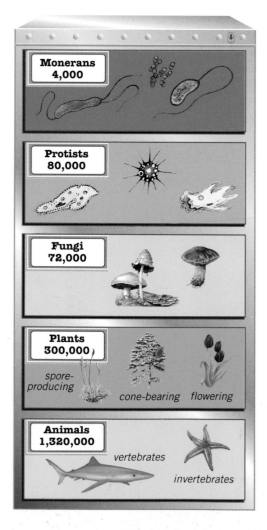

Monerans
4,000

Protists
80,000

Fungi
72,000

Plants
300,000

spore-producing    cone-bearing    flowering

Animals
1,320,000

vertebrates

invertebrates

# Animals

There are millions of different types of animal. Some are huge but others are tiny and can only be seen under a microscope.

Animals cannot make their own food like plants can. All animals have to eat plants or other animals.

A cheetah chasing a gazelle. Cheetahs are the world's fastest land animals.

## Warm-blooded animals

Birds and mammals can control their body temperature. This is called being warm-blooded. The animal's body stays at the same temperature no matter how hot or cold its surroundings are.

Warm-blooded animals use lots of energy keeping warm so they must eat a lot of food.

## Cold-blooded animals

The body temperature of a cold-blooded animal changes when the temperature of its surroundings changes. Its blood will be warm or cold depending on the temperature around it. Cold-blooded animals use the Sun's heat to warm up. Lizards are cold-blooded animals.

## Movement

Animals must move around to find food. Most have muscles and a skeleton to do this. Most animals also have some kind of brain to control their bodies and help them move.

 Anemones are animals, although they look like plants.

## Vertebrates

A vertebrate is an animal with a backbone. Most bigger animals, such as fishes, reptiles, birds, and mammals, are vertebrates.

## Invertebrates

An invertebrate is an animal without a backbone. Insects, snails, and worms are invertebrates. Invertebrates sometimes have a hard shell or an outer skeleton. Others, such as jellyfish, are supported by the water around them.

### FAST FACTS

☐ Scientists have named 1.5 million different species of animal. More than one million of these animals are insects.

☐ The five groups of vertebrates include about 50,000 species.

This frog has an internal skeleton and a backbone. It is a vertebrate.

This scorpion has a skeleton on the outside of its body and no backbone. It is an invertebrate.

Fishes, amphibians, reptiles, birds, and mammals are all vertebrates.

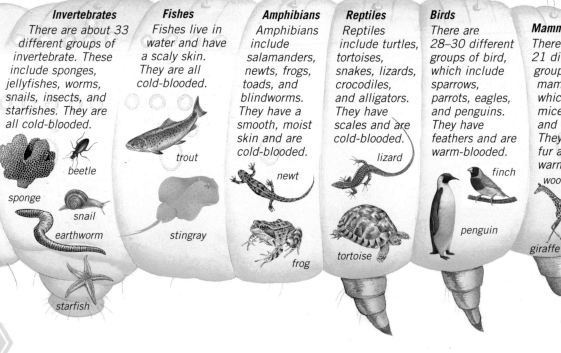

**Invertebrates**
There are about 33 different groups of invertebrate. These include sponges, jellyfishes, worms, snails, insects, and starfishes. They are all cold-blooded.

beetle

sponge

snail

earthworm

starfish

**Fishes**
Fishes live in water and have a scaly skin. They are all cold-blooded.

trout

stingray

**Amphibians**
Amphibians include salamanders, newts, frogs, toads, and blindworms. They have a smooth, moist skin and are cold-blooded.

newt

frog

**Reptiles**
Reptiles include turtles, tortoises, snakes, lizards, crocodiles, and alligators. They have scales and are cold-blooded.

lizard

tortoise

**Birds**
There are 28–30 different groups of bird, which include sparrows, parrots, eagles, and penguins. They have feathers and are warm-blooded.

finch

penguin

**Mammals**
There are 21 different groups of mammal, which include mice, bats, and bears. They have fur and are warm-blooded.

woodmouse

giraffe

# Plants

Plants are very successful living things. They have existed on the Earth for longer than animals. They can make their own food. Without plants, all animals, including humans, would die.

## Food factories

Plants take in carbon dioxide gas from the air through their leaves. They take up water from the soil through their roots. Leaves absorb (soak up) sunlight and use this to turn the carbon dioxide and water into sugars (food) for the plant. This process is called photosynthesis. During photosynthesis, plants release oxygen gas into the air.

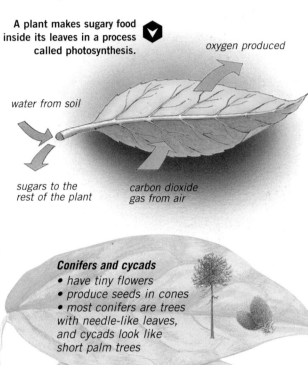

A plant makes sugary food inside its leaves in a process called photosynthesis.

oxygen produced

water from soil

sugars to the rest of the plant

carbon dioxide gas from air

**Mosses and liverworts**
• live in damp places
• produce spores (tiny, dust-like particles) instead of seeds
• most have no roots

**Ferns**
• live in damp places
• produce spores instead of seeds
• have leaves called fronds and fine roots

**Conifers and cycads**
• have tiny flowers
• produce seeds in cones
• most conifers are trees with needle-like leaves, and cycads look like short palm trees

**Flowering plants**
• produce flowers and seeds
• are the most common plants

Plants are divided into four main groups.

## Roots and stems

A plant has roots to anchor it in the ground. The roots take up water and minerals from the soil. A stem joins the roots to the leaves and holds the plant upright. Stems also hold the leaves up so that the leaves can collect sunshine for photosynthesis.

## FAST FACTS

**The four plant groups:**
☐ Mosses and liverworts: 16,000 different types
☐ Ferns: 10,000 different types
☐ Conifers (plants with cones): 500 different types
☐ Flowering plants: 250,000 different types. More than 80 per cent of plants are flowering plants.

 Some redwood trees are as tall as the American Statue of Liberty.

## Spore plants

Ferns, mosses, and liverworts do not make seeds. Instead, they make spores, which are dust-like particles. Spores can grow into new plants.

## Pollination

Pollination is when pollen is carried from one flower to another. Flowering plants make pollen, which contain the male sex cells.

Insects and birds go to flowers to drink nectar. They carry away pollen on their bodies. Other flowers, such as grasses, use the wind to carry their pollen.

## Fertilization

If the pollen reaches another flower, the pollen may join together with the female sex cell. This is fertilization. A seed will form.

## Seeds

A seed contains the tiny beginnings of a plant. Seeds can stay dormant (asleep) for years before growing. This helps them to survive cold weather or very dry conditions. When conditions are good, the seed may grow into a new plant.

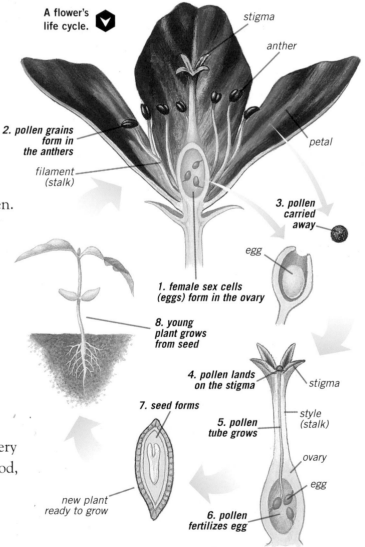

A flower's life cycle.

stigma

anther

petal

2. pollen grains form in the anthers

filament (stalk)

3. pollen carried away

egg

1. female sex cells (eggs) form in the ovary

8. young plant grows from seed

4. pollen lands on the stigma

stigma

7. seed forms

style (stalk)

5. pollen tube grows

ovary

egg

6. pollen fertilizes egg

new plant ready to grow

# Birds

There are nearly 9,000 different species of bird. They range from the tiny, bee-sized hummingbird to the giant ostrich.

Birds are different from other animals because they have feathers. They have wings instead of arms and most are fast and powerful fliers.

A small bird such as the blue tit has about 3,000 feathers.

**DID YOU KNOW?**

Ducks and geese hatch out with fluffy feathers. They can run around almost straight away and feed themselves.

Not all birds fly. Penguins use their wings for swimming instead of flying.

## Feeding

Flying uses up lots of energy, so birds must eat plenty of food. Some birds are vegetarians, eating fruit, seeds, nuts, or leaves. Many are meat-eaters and eat fish, insects, worms, frogs, birds, and other small animals.

## Feathered fliers

Most birds are excellent flying machines. Their bones are hollow, which makes them very light. The feathers of a bird give it a smooth shape, which helps it to slip easily through the air.

A bird's wings are curved. This helps to lift the bird up into the air. Powerful chest muscles beat the wings up and down.

barb

stem

barbules

A feather is made up of a central stem with side barbs (branches). The barbs are linked together.

## Birds of prey

Birds of prey, such as owls, hunt for their food. Owls fly almost silently as they search for food. They have excellent hearing. When they pick up the sound of a mouse, they swoop down. Strong talons (claws) snatch the mouse from the ground.

## Nests

Birds build nests in trees and bushes. They collect twigs to make the nest and some birds line the nest with their own feathers.

Ovenbirds and weaver birds build unusual nests. Ovenbirds make a strong nest the size of a football out of mud and cow dung. Weaver birds make their nests by weaving together pieces of grass.

An ovenbird in its round nest.

A weaver bird in its grassy nest.

## Beaks

Different birds have beaks of different shapes and sizes. The curlew has a long beak to find worms hidden deep in the mud. The pelican catches fish in its stretchy throat pouch. The flamingo uses its beak as a sieve to take tiny creatures from the water. The eagle tears the flesh of its prey with its hooked beak. The hawfinch uses its short, strong beak to crack seeds.

curlew

pelican

hawfinch

flamingo

eagle

## Mating

Male birds are usually more colourful than females. The males often sing or perform acrobatics to impress females. If the female likes what she sees, she may mate with the male.

After mating, birds lay eggs. Many baby birds are naked when they hatch from the eggs. They stay safe and warm inside a nest while they grow their feathers.

Male frigate birds have a red throat sac that they use to impress females.

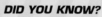

**DID YOU KNOW?**

*Some scientists think that birds – including the birds in your garden – may be the direct descendants of the dinosaurs.*

# Fishes

Fishes have existed on Earth for nearly 400 million years. Today there are more than 25,000 different species of fish.

## Scales and gills

A fish has a backbone that supports its body. The outside of a fish is coated with hard, slippery scales. The shape of a fish's body and its scales help it to slip easily through water.

Most fishes breathe through gills. Gills take oxygen gas from the water. Fishes are cold-blooded. This means that their body temperature changes with the temperature of their surroundings.

Mudskippers can breathe in air as well as in water. They crawl over the mud using their stiff fins like crutches.

## Fish life cycles

Most fishes lay lots of very small eggs. However, a few, such as many sharks, give birth to live young. Some eggs float in the sea. Others stick to plants and rocks. Most fishes do not take care of their young.

### DID YOU KNOW?

The sailfish is probably the fastest fish in the sea. It can swim at 110 kilometres (68 miles) per hour. That is as fast as a cheetah can sprint on land.

A sailfish has a powerful tail to help it swim fast.

Bony fishes are covered with thin, overlapping scales. Bony fishes pump water over the gills by opening and closing the mouth.

### FAST FACTS

**Types of fish:**

☐ Bony fish – 95 per cent of fish are bony fishes, including tuna, goldfish, trout, and salmon. Their skeletons are made of bone.

☐ Cartilaginous fish – Sharks, rays, skates are cartilaginous fishes. Their skeletons are made of tough cartilage.

fin

gill cover removed to show gills

gill cover

fin

fin

scaly body

# Mammals

There are about 4,000 different species of mammal. They live all over the world, from icy polar regions to baking deserts and tropical rainforests.

Mammals are warm-blooded. Their bodies stay at the same high temperature whatever the temperature around them.

 A seal pup feeds on its mother's rich milk. It helps the pup to grow quickly.

## Mammal features

Humans, cats, elephants, and whales are all mammals. Mammals are usually more intelligent than other animals and are the only animals to have fur or hair.

The young of most mammals are born live. However, a few mammals lay eggs. Females feed their young on milk.

## Mammal groups

Mammals are divided into three groups, depending on how their young develop.

• Placental mammals – These mammals give birth to well-developed young. Inside the mother's body, the young get nutrients through a special organ called the placenta.

**Egg-laying mammals**

**Monotremes**
platypuses, echidnas

*platypus*

**Live-bearing mammals**

**Marsupials**
kangaroos, wallabies, koalas, possums

*kangaroo*

**Placental mammals**

**Insectivores**
hedgehogs, shrews, moles

*hedgehog*

**Bats**
fruit bats, mouse-tailed bats, horseshoe bats

*bat*

**Edentates**
anteaters, sloths, armadillos

*giant anteater*

**Primates**
lemurs, monkeys, apes, humans

*orang-utan*

**Carnivores**
dogs and foxes, bears, pandas, weasels, raccoons, cats

*weasel*

**DID YOU KNOW?**

The largest order of mammals is the rodents. There are 1,700 rodent species.

 Mammals are divided into 21 orders (groups). The main orders are shown here.

- Marsupials – These mammals give birth to tiny young. The young finish their development in a pouch on their mother's body.

- Monotremes – These mammals hatch out of eggs.

## Sky and sea

Bats are the only mammals that can fly. There are hundreds of different bats. They make up one quarter of all mammal species. A bat's wings are made of thin flaps of skin stretched between long finger bones.

Sea mammals include whales, dolphins, and seals. Dolphins and whales spend their whole lives in the sea. Seals, sea lions, and walruses come out of the sea to breed (have young).

## Teeth

Most mammals have three types of teeth: incisors, canines, and molars. Incisors are at the very front of the mouth and are used for cutting. Canines are pointed and are used for gripping and tearing. Molars are towards the back of the mouth and are used for grinding up food.

You can see the sharp canine teeth clearly in this lion's mouth.

**Pinnipedes**
seals, walruses, sea lions

*walrus*

**Proboscids**
elephants

*elephant*

**Even-toed ungulates**
pigs, camels, deer, giraffes, cattle

*red deer*

**Rodents**
squirrels, mice, beavers, rats, voles, chipmunks, porcupines

*chipmunk*

**Odd-toed ungulates**
horses, tapirs, rhinoceroses

**Whales**
dolphins, porpoises, whales

*blue whale*

*rhinoceros*

*hare*

**Lagomorphs**
rabbits, hares, pikas

# Amphibians

Toads, frogs, salamanders, and newts are amphibians. Most amphibians live partly on land and partly in the water.

Amphibians have loose, moist skin and usually live in damp places. Young amphibians often look very different from their parents. A tadpole looks nothing like a frog!

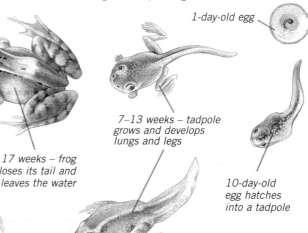

The fire salamander's skin is so poisonous that it can kill small mammals.

## Salamanders and newts

Most salamanders and newts are small and secretive. They feed on slow-moving animals such as snails, slugs, and worms. Giant salamanders can grow up to 1.6 metres (5.2 feet) long!

## Toads and frogs

Like salamanders and newts, toads and frogs are also meat-eaters. They catch food on their long, sticky tongues.

A frog has three stages in its life cycle – egg, tadpole, and adult frog.

1-day-old egg

7–13 weeks – tadpole grows and develops lungs and legs

17 weeks – frog loses its tail and leaves the water

10-day-old egg hatches into a tadpole

## Caecilians

Caecilians look more like worms than amphibians. They wriggle through the damp soils of tropical forests. They eat worms, termites, and lizards.

Caecilians use their heads like garden trowels to dig in the mud for food.

# Reptiles

Snakes, lizards, crocodiles, alligators, and turtles are all reptiles. They have scaly, dry skin and they lay eggs.

Some reptiles live on land and some live in water. All reptiles breathe air.

## Cold-blooded

Reptiles usually live in warm places. They are cold-blooded and need the Sun's heat to warm their bodies. Reptiles can live in dry places. They have a scaly skin that stops their bodies from drying out as they bask in the sunshine.

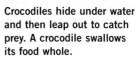
Crocodiles hide under water and then leap out to catch prey. A crocodile swallows its food whole.

A chameleon shoots out its tongue to catch an insect.

## Waterproof eggs

The main difference between amphibians and reptiles is where they lay their eggs. Reptiles lay their eggs on land and amphibians lay their eggs in water. Even reptiles that live in water, such as crocodiles and turtles, lay their eggs on land.

Cobras rear up and then lunge forward to bite their prey.

## Snakes

Snakes are an unusual group of reptiles. They have no legs or eyelids, and no ears on the outside of their bodies.

Some snakes use venom (poison) for attacking others or defending themselves. Other snakes kill by squeezing animals tightly in their strong coils.

# Invertebrates

Animals without backbones are called invertebrates. Ninety-nine per cent of all animals are invertebrates. They live all over the world – in the sea, in fresh water, and on land. They include sponges, worms, starfishes, snails, insects, and crabs.

 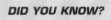
### Squid

Squid live in the ocean. They are the fastest swimming invertebrates. Squid are also the largest invertebrates. Giant squid can grow up to 18 metres (60 feet) long.

Squid protect themselves from predators by squirting black ink into the water. The ink hides the squid as it quickly swims away from danger.

Squid are meat-eaters. >

## Skeleton on the outside

Many invertebrates have hard skeletons on the outside of their bodies. The skeleton acts as a suit of armour that protects the soft body inside.

The skeleton is often divided into sections. This allows the animal to twist, turn, and squirm.

## Molluscs

Snails, slugs, and shellfish belong to a group called molluscs. Some, such as snails and slugs, have a large muscular foot. They use the foot for walking or swimming.

Oysters and mussels live in water. Their shells are made of two parts joined together. They get their food by straining tiny particles from the water.

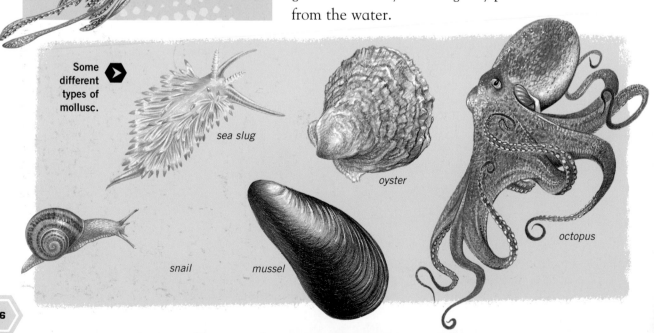

Some different types of mollusc. >

sea slug

oyster

octopus

snail

mussel

## Arachnids

Spiders and scorpions are not insects. They belong to a group called arachnids. They have eight legs and most of them live on land.

There are 30,000 species of spider and almost 1,000 species of scorpion. A scorpion uses the sting at the end of its tail to stun its prey.

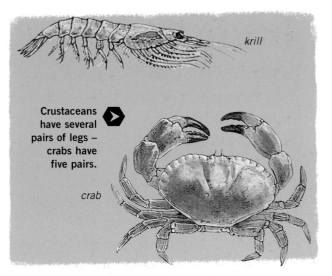

krill

**Crustaceans have several pairs of legs – crabs have five pairs.**

crab

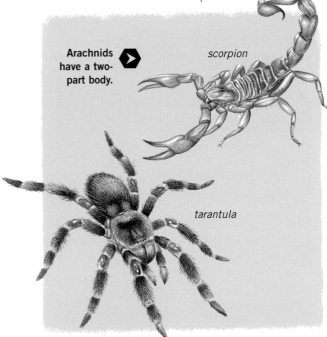

**Arachnids have a two-part body.**

scorpion

tarantula

## Crustaceans

Crabs, lobsters, prawns, and woodlice belong to a group called crustaceans. All crustaceans have a hard shell. Most live in water but some, such as woodlice, live on land. There are around 150,000 species of crustacean.

## Insects

There are over one million species of insect. All insects have six legs. Most have wings and one pair of antennae (feelers).

## Starfish and sea urchins

Starfish and sea urchins belong to a group called echinoderms. The word echinoderm means 'spiny-skinned'. Most echinoderms have lots of small tube-feet with suckers on the end.

An echinoderm's body is usually made up of five parts. These are arranged like the spokes of a wheel.

**A starfish's mouth is underneath its body. It must crawl over the food it wants to eat.**

# Insects

Insects are invertebrates, which means that they have no backbone. All insects have a hard outer casing and three main body parts – a head, thorax, and abdomen.

## Small is good

Most insects are less than 2.5 centimetres (1 inch) long. Their small size allows insects to live in small spaces and survive on very little food.

The smallest insects are fairy flies. They are less than a quarter of the size of a pinhead. The largest insects are not much bigger than an adult's hand.

▼ A typical insect, such as a wasp, has six legs and three parts to its body.

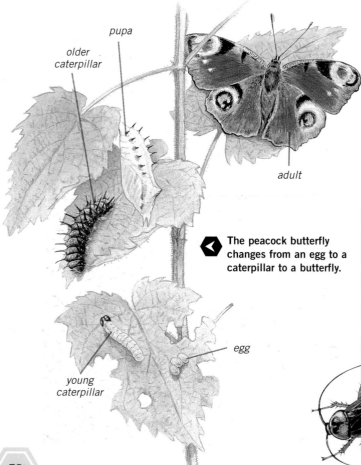

pupa

older caterpillar

adult

◀ The peacock butterfly changes from an egg to a caterpillar to a butterfly.

egg

young caterpillar

## Changing states

A butterfly begins life as a caterpillar. As it grows, it changes completely to become a butterfly. This change is called complete metamorphosis.

Other insects look like their parents when they hatch. As they develop, they get bigger and grow wings. This change is called incomplete metamorphosis.

## Cockroaches

Cockroaches have lived on Earth for about 300 million years – since before the dinosaurs. Cockroaches eat almost anything, including glue, paper, soap, ink, and shoe polish. They can even live for three months on just water.

◀ Cockroaches are a very successful and tough insect.

# Bacteria and viruses

Bacteria and viruses are microbes – tiny living things that can only be seen under a microscope.

Most bacteria are harmless and some can even be useful. Bacteria inside your digestive system help you digest (take the goodness from) food. Other microbes are harmful and can cause disease

## Bacteria

Most bacteria are made of just one cell. A bacterium is about 1,000 times smaller than an animal cell. The outer coating of a bacterium is slimy and is sometimes covered with tiny hairs. Longer strands called flagella help the bacterium to move around.

 Bacteria move around using their long flagella.

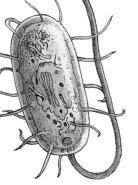

**DID YOU KNOW?**

Your body is carrying over 100,000 billion bacteria.

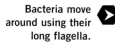 **FAST FACTS**

**Diseases caused by bacteria:**
☐ cholera, tetanus, typhoid, food poisoning
**Diseases caused by viruses:**
☐ common cold, influenza, Aids, measles

The influenza virus causes the patient to have a high temperature, aches, and tiredness.

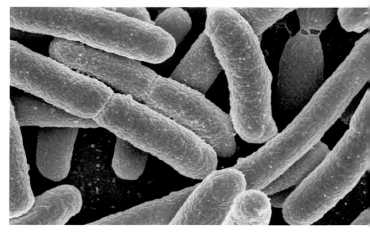

These bacteria are dividing. A bacterium can divide in two once every 30 minutes.

## Viruses

Viruses are even smaller than bacteria. They are not made up of cells and they are not true living things. They cannot grow and reproduce on their own. Instead, they come to life inside other living things.

## Food poisoning

Bacteria can grow on food. If we eat these bacteria they can give us food poisoning. They cause us to be sick and have diarrhoea.

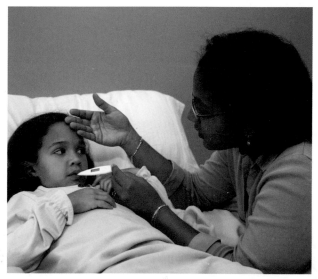

# Polar life

The North Pole is surrounded by the frozen Arctic Ocean. The South Pole is surrounded by a frozen continent – Antarctica.

Even though it is so cold, plants and animals live at the North and South Poles. They have found ways to survive the harsh conditions.

## Polar plants

To keep out of the icy winds, polar plants grow close to the ground. In the short summer, plants burst into flower and quickly produce seeds. Many of these seeds survive the winter buried in the soil.

Plants provide food for the animals that visit the Arctic tundra (treeless land) in summer to have their young.

▼ Musk oxen live on the Arctic tundra all year round. If they are attacked by wolves, they form a circle with the young in the middle.

▼ Low-growing flowers cover the Arctic tundra in summer.

## Polar animals

Polar animals have thick fur or feathers to keep in their body heat. Their fur or feathers often turn white in winter for camouflage against the snow.

Many animals have a thick layer of fat under their skin. This traps body heat and acts as an energy store when food is hard to find.

## The Arctic tern

Every year, a small bird called the Arctic tern makes an amazing journey. It travels more than 35,000 kilometres (22,000 miles) from one end of the world to the other, and back again. It makes this journey to escape the freezing winter weather at both of the Poles.

► Polar bears live on the Arctic ice.

▼ Arctic tern

# Desert life

Deserts can be boiling hot or freezing cold, but they are all very dry. Some animals and plants can survive in deserts. All of them must find ways to get water.

## Desert plants

The roots of some desert plants grow deep into the ground to find water. Others spread out just under the surface of the ground, but over a wide area. As soon as it rains, they soak up as much water as possible.

Cacti are a type of desert plant. They store water in their stems or leaves.

◀ Elf owls shelter and nest inside holes in giant cacti.

▼ Camels can go for several weeks without water.

## Desert animals

Small animals escape the Sun's heat by hiding underground during the day. They only come out at night when it is cooler.

Most desert animals do not need much water. The kangaroo rat does not drink at all. It gets water from its food. Camels store fat in their humps. They can break down this fat to provide them with energy and water.

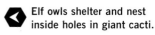

## Fennec fox

The large ears of the African fennec fox can be up to 15 centimetres (6 inches) long. They give off heat like a radiator. This helps to keep the fox cool.

◀ Reptiles, such as the frilled lizard, are common in deserts. Their skin keeps in water and they can go for a long time without food.

# Ocean life

The oceans cover almost three-quarters of the Earth's surface. They are home to a huge variety of plants and animals.

Most living things are found in the top 100 metres (330 feet) of the oceans. Below this there is very little sunlight, which most plants and animals need to survive.

## Floating food

Tiny plants and animals called plankton float around in the oceans. Fish, birds, and huge whales feed on the masses of plankton.

## Coral reefs

Coral reefs form over thousands of years. They are made from the skeletons of tiny ocean animals called corals. They form in warm, shallow waters and are home to more than a third of all fish species. Many other ocean creatures also live there such as starfish, anemones, eels, jellyfish, and crabs.

Porcupine fish live on coral reefs. They swallow water and swell up if they are in danger. This makes their sharp spines stick out.

Waters around coral reefs are full of life.

moray eel

manta ray

jellyfish

clown fish

trumpet fish

crab

damsel fish

parrot fish

starfish

seahorse

sea anemone

Many larger animals live in the open ocean. Smaller fish, such as anchovies, live near coasts.

Bottom-dwelling animals often stay in one place and wait for their food to come to them.

turtle

tuna

bull shark

anchovy

hatchet fish

## Life in the depths

In deep water, animals have to cope with pitch darkness and cold. The weight of the water pushing down on them is huge – it would easily crush a human.

Deep-ocean animals feed on each other, or on the dead animals, food scraps, and droppings that fall from the surface waters.

brittle star

angler fish

# Animal behaviour

Almost anything an animal does is a type of behaviour. Chimpanzees digging for termites, lion cubs playing, wasps building a nest – all these are examples of animal behaviour.

In a wolf pack, each wolf knows its place.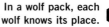

## Automatic behaviour

When animals are born, they already know how to do certain things. Spiders know how to spin a web. A human baby knows how to suck, which means that the baby is able to feed from its mother straight away.

These behaviours are automatic or in-built . They are passed down from one generation to the next.

### BIOGRAPHY

**Konrad Lorenz**

Konrad Lorenz (1903–1989) was one of the first scientists to study animal behaviour. He noticed that during the first few hours of an animal's life, it learns to recognize its parents. Some young geese treated Lorenz as their 'mother' because he was the first thing they saw when they hatched.

Male bighorn sheep fight to decide who is the strongest. Their fights are head-butting contests.

## Learned behaviour

Not all behaviours are automatic. Other behaviours must be learned. Young animals learn behaviours from their parents.

Young chimpanzees watch their mothers use plant stems to get termites out of a termite mound. Over many years, the young chimps learn this behaviour.

Chimps are very intelligent. They use tools to get their food.

## Communication

Animals use behaviour to communicate with (send messages to) other animals. They can send messages using sounds, smells, or movements. Female fireflies even use patterns of flashing lights to attract a mate.

## Surviving the seasons

Different behaviours help animals to survive bad weather. Some birds, mammals, fishes, and insects migrate (make long journeys). They do this to avoid bad weather or poor food supplies. Others migrate to find a safe place to have their young.

Some animals survive bad weather by going into a deep sleep. Surviving cold conditions like this is called hibernation.

These butterflies are hibernating on Mexican pine trees. Monarch butterflies migrate from Canada to Mexico for the winter – a journey of 4,000 kilometres (2,480 miles).

## Termite mounds

Millions of termites live together in a termite mound. The termites work together to build the mound out of soil stuck together with saliva and droppings.

Different types of termite live in the mound. Each type of termite has its own special job to do. If people built on the same scale as termites, their towers would be over one kilometre (0.6 miles) high.

In a termite mound there is a king, queen, and many soldiers and workers.

king

queen

alates (termites that mate and fly away to become the king and queen of a new mound)

soldiers (protect the mound from attack)

workers (collect food and build the nest)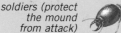

# Ecology

Ecology is the study of how living things depend on each other for survival. Ecologists try to discover the links between plants, animals, and their surroundings.

## Food chains and webs

Plants use energy from sunlight and water from the soil to make their own food. Animals cannot make their own food – they have to eat plants or other animals.

A food chain is the path that food follows through a plant to two or more animals. Most animals eat several types of food. They are part of a complicated food web, instead of a simple food chain.

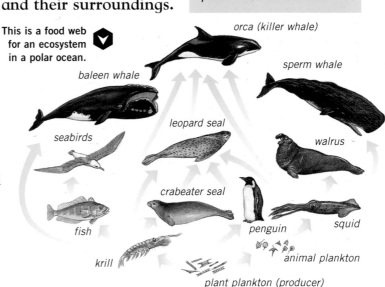

This is a food web for an ecosystem in a polar ocean.

orca (killer whale)
sperm whale
baleen whale
leopard seal
seabirds
walrus
crabeater seal
penguin
squid
fish
krill
animal plankton
plant plankton (producer)

## Biomes and ecosystems

A biome is a large area that is home to certain animals and plants. Forests, deserts, and grasslands are biomes.

Biomes are divided into different ecosystems. In a forest biome there could be a wood of oak trees and a wood of pine trees. Each wood is an ecosystem.

## Communities

In an ecosystem, communities (groups) of animals and plants live in a particular habitat. The high branches of a tree or the forest floor are habitats.

Animals and plants in a community can help each other. Wood ants feed on leaf-eating insects. This helps the trees to keep more of their leaves.

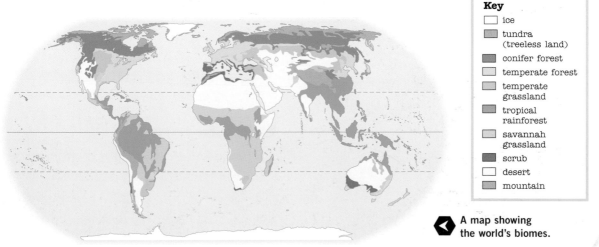

**Key**
- ice
- tundra (treeless land)
- conifer forest
- temperate forest
- temperate grassland
- tropical rainforest
- savannah grassland
- scrub
- desert
- mountain

**A map showing the world's biomes.**

# Life

The Earth formed around 4,600 million years ago. The early Earth was a hot and dangerous place with many volcanoes. Life on Earth started around 3,500 million years ago.

Today, every part of our planet is full of life. From bacteria to whales, trees to algae, life is everywhere.

## What is life?

All living things have certain things in common. They feed and they get rid of waste. They react to the world around them. They also make new versions of themselves.

## How did life start?

Scientists do not know for certain how life started. They think that energy from the Sun and lightning strikes may have helped form special chemicals. These chemicals were able to copy themselves. This was the start of life.

**Timeline of the history of life on Earth.** ▶

*mya = millions of years ago*

CRETACEOUS

many turtles and crocodiles

TRIASSIC

first dinosaurs

250 mya
great extinction kills more than half of all living things

earliest snakes

modern bony fishes

PERMIAN

early sea reptiles

290 mya

412 mya

DEVONIAN

insects invade land

early ferns

first amphibians

SILURIAN

435 mya

first reptiles

360 mya

jawed fishes

winged insects

first ammonites (shellfishes)

first land plants

early jellyfishes

550 mya explosion of new life forms

CARBONIFEROUS

ORDOVICIAN

jawless fishes

first trilobites

CAMBRIAN

500 mya

first bacteria (3,500 mya)

Earth forms (4,600 mya)

## First life forms

The first life forms were tiny creatures similar to bacteria. They were made of just one cell. For over 2,000 million years these were the only life forms on Earth.

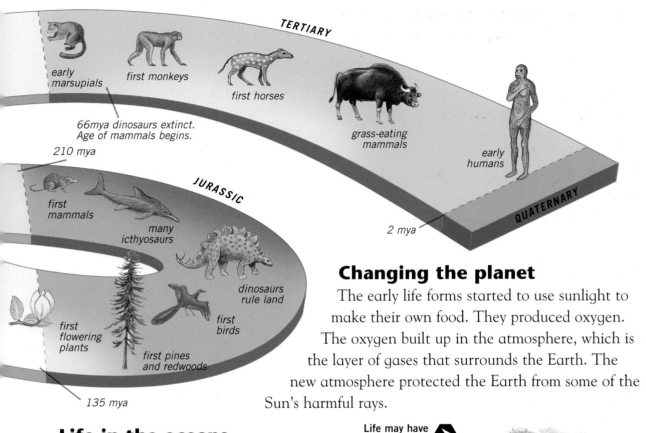

TERTIARY

early marsupials

first monkeys

first horses

grass-eating mammals

early humans

QUATERNARY

66mya dinosaurs extinct. Age of mammals begins.

210 mya

JURASSIC

first mammals

many icthyosaurs

dinosaurs rule land

first birds

first flowering plants

first pines and redwoods

135 mya

2 mya

## Changing the planet

The early life forms started to use sunlight to make their own food. They produced oxygen. The oxygen built up in the atmosphere, which is the layer of gases that surrounds the Earth. The new atmosphere protected the Earth from some of the Sun's harmful rays.

## Life in the oceans

Around 600 million years ago, ocean life began to develop more rapidly. Simple animals that looked like jellyfishes or worms developed into animals with backbones. This included the first fishes. This development took hundreds of millions of years.

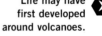
Life may have first developed around volcanoes.

## Life on land

About 400 million years ago, life moved on to the land. Plants grew on the land. Next came the insects and other small animals. Over time, 'walking fishes' developed. These were amphibians.

Amphibians developed into the first large land animals: the reptiles. Dinosaurs were reptiles. Later, birds and mammals developed. Humans are a type of mammal.

### DID YOU KNOW?

*If we imagine the history of the Earth happening in 12 hours starting at 12 noon, simple bacteria would appear after 3 hours, at 3pm. The first worms and jellyfishes would appear at about 10pm. The first dinosaurs would appear at 11.45pm. Humans would not appear until one minute before midnight!*

# Evolution

Evolution is the gradual change in living things over millions of years. Evolution causes new species (types) of living thing to develop.

## Natural selection

Planet Earth changes gradually over time. It can become warmer, cooler, wetter, or drier. Some living things can survive these changes. Those that can survive may have offspring. The features that helped the parents to survive are passed to the offspring.

This idea is called natural selection or 'the survival of the fittest'. Evolution happens because of natural selection.

## Evidence for evolution

Fossils are the remains of living things that formed over millions of years. Scientists can work out how old fossils are. Fossils help scientists to find out about evolution. Fossils have shown us that amphibians evolved from fishes, and that birds evolved from reptiles.

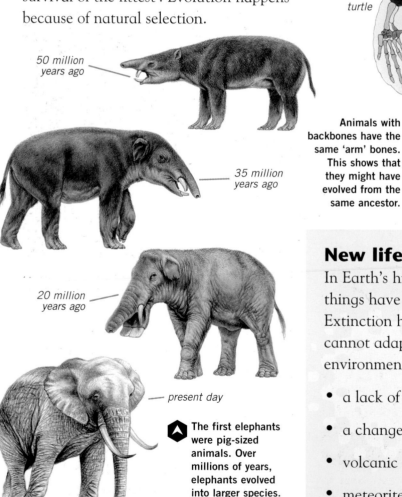

50 million years ago

35 million years ago

20 million years ago

present day

turtle

human

bird

**Animals with backbones have the same 'arm' bones. This shows that they might have evolved from the same ancestor.**

▲ **The first elephants were pig-sized animals. Over millions of years, elephants evolved into larger species.**

## New life for old

In Earth's history, millions of living things have become extinct (died out). Extinction happens when a living thing cannot adapt to changes in the environment such as:

- a lack of food

- a change in the climate

- volcanic eruptions

- meteorites (big rocks from space) hitting the Earth.

# Astronomy

On a clear, dark night it is possible to see about 4,000 stars in the sky. Our Sun and all these stars belong to our Milky Way galaxy. There are billions of other galaxies in the universe.

Astronomy is the study of the stars, planets, galaxies, and the rest of the universe.

## Telescopes for astronomy

Astronomers use telescopes to look into space. Some telescopes detect light from faraway objects. Other telescopes detect heat or radio waves from faraway objects.

Information from telescopes tells atronomers how hot stars are, what gas clouds are made of, and how fast galaxies are moving.

You can learn about the night sky with the naked eye, a pair of binoculars, or a telescope.

*BIOGRAPHY*

**Nicolaus Copernicus**
Astronomer Nicolaus Copernicus was born in Poland in 1473. At that time, most people thought that the Sun, the Moon, and the planets travelled around the Earth. Copernicus realized that the Earth and other planets actually travel around the Sun.

This picture was taken over several hours. The trails of light are made by the stars. The stars appear to move round in the sky because the Earth spins once a day.

## Astronomy as a hobby

You don't need a telescope to discover the night sky. Learn some of the constellations. Then you can spot planets and watch for meteors (shooting stars).

You can also use a pair of binoculars to look at the night sky. You will be able to see the craters on the Moon, and the stars in the Milky Way.

# Sun

The Sun is our very own star. It is a gigantic ball of glowing gases.

The Sun gives us light and warmth. Most life on Earth needs energy from the Sun to grow and to survive.

sunspots

## Inside the Sun

The Sun is mostly made of hydrogen gas. Inside the Sun, hydrogen gas changes to helium gas (the gas used to fill party balloons). This change produces heat and light.

The Sun is constantly changing. The dark patches are sunspots. Sunspots look dark because they are cooler.

## The surface of the Sun

The yellow surface of the Sun is called the photosphere. It seems to bubble like a cauldron as hot gas comes to the surface. The photosphere is surrounded by the Sun's atmosphere. The atmosphere is made of thin, very hot gas that we do not normally see.

## FAST FACTS

**Sun facts**
- ☐ Diameter: 1.4 million km (870,000 miles)
- ☐ Mass: 333,000 times Earth's mass
- ☐ Temperature at the surface: 5,500°C (9,930°F)
- ☐ Temperature at the centre: 15 million°C (27 million°F)
- ☐ Average distance from Earth: 150 million km (93 million miles)

## Solar flares

Sometimes, huge flares explode at the surface of the Sun. They blast gas far into space. The gas travels to Earth and beyond. These solar flares can affect radio communications on Earth. They are also dangerous for astronauts working in space.

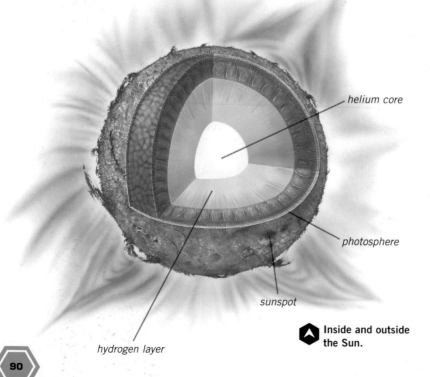

helium core

photosphere

sunspot

hydrogen layer

Inside and outside the Sun.

### DID YOU KNOW?

*Warning! Do not look at the Sun, even through sunglasses. You could permanently damage your eyesight.*

# Orbits

An orbit is a path around a central point. The path can
be circular or oval. The Moon travels in an orbit around
the Earth. The Earth and other planets travel in orbits
around the Sun.

The Moon never
stops moving
around our planet.

## A central pull

Gravity is a pulling force. The Earth's
gravity pulls on the Moon. This keeps
the Moon moving in its orbit. If the Earth
had no gravity, the Moon would fly off
into space.

## Reaching orbit

Rockets launch satellites and spacecraft
into space. To stay in an orbit around the
Earth, they must reach a speed of 28,000
kilometres (17,400 miles) per hour. If they
are not fast enough, they will crash back
to Earth.

◄ This photo of the
International Space
Station (ISS) was taken
from another spacecraft.
The ISS is in orbit
around the Earth.

The blue arrow shows
the orbit of the ball. ▶

## Experience an orbit

Tie an object firmly to a piece of string. Go to an open space and
whirl it around. You are pulling on the string to keep the object in
an orbit around your hand.

Your hand is like the Earth. The string is like the Earth's gravity
pulling on the object. The object is like the Moon orbiting the Earth.

# Solar System

Our Solar System is made up of the Sun and the planets that travel around it. Compared to the Earth, the Solar System is huge. Compared to the rest of the universe, the Solar System is a tiny speck.

## The planets

Eight major planets orbit the Sun. They are the main members of the Solar System. Six of the planets have moons. There are more than 60 moons altogether in the Solar System.

Pluto used to be called a planet. Today, scientists call Pluto a dwarf planet. It travels further from the Sun than the eight major planets.

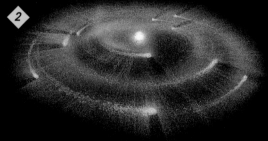

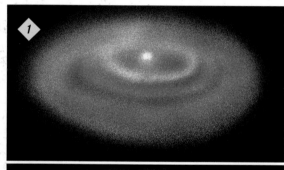

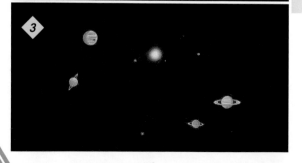

## The formation of the Solar System

The Solar System first formed about 4,600 million years ago.

1. The brand new Sun was surrounded by a huge disc of gas and dust.

2. Material in the disc began to clump together.

3. After millions of years, the largest clumps had become the planets. Comets, asteroids, and meteoroids are the smaller, leftover pieces.

## Rocky planets

Mercury, Venus, Earth, and Mars are the planets nearest the Sun. They are small and rocky. You can see Venus from the Earth. It looks very bright and is found in the west, just after sunset.

## Gas giants

Jupiter and Saturn are giant gas planets. Jupiter is covered with colourful, swirling clouds and is 11 times larger than the Earth.

Saturn is surrounded by rings. The rings are made from swarms of icy chunks. They range from pieces the size of a golf ball up to boulders the size of a house.

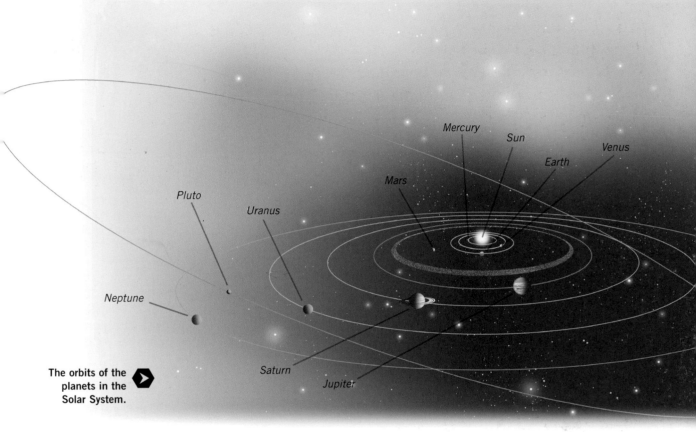

The orbits of the planets in the Solar System.

## Icy planets

Uranus and Neptune are made of gas and ice. At the north and south poles on Uranus, night and day each last 42 years. This is because the planet is tilted on its side and the poles point away from the Sun for 42 years. Pluto is tiny and is made of rock and ice.

### FAST FACTS

**The orbits of the main planets and Pluto**

| Planet | Average distance from Sun (million km) | Time taken to orbit Sun (to nearest Earth day/year) |
| --- | --- | --- |
| Mercury | 58 | 88 days |
| Venus | 108 | 225 days |
| Earth | 150 | 365 days |
| Mars | 228 | 687 days |
| Jupiter | 778 | 12 years |
| Saturn | 1,427 | 30 years |
| Uranus | 2,860 | 84 years |
| Neptune | 4,500 | 165 years |
| Pluto | 4,435 (nearest), 7,372 (farthest) | 248 years |

# Asteroids and comets

Asteroids are rocky chunks that travel around the Sun. Most of them travel in the asteroid belt, which is a long way from the Sun, between Mars and Jupiter.

Comets are mainly made of ice. Sometimes you can see long tails stretching out behind a comet.

## Asteroids

Millions of asteroids orbit (travel around) the Sun. Though there are so many, all these small rocky chunks together would be much smaller than our Moon.

Asteroids are made of rock, metal, or a mixture of both. They are small pieces left over from when the planet formed 4,600 million years ago.

## Comets

Though comets look spectacular, they contain very little material. The Earth has passed through the tail of a comet without any noticeable effect. Only the middle of a comet is solid. It is made of a mixture of ice and dust.

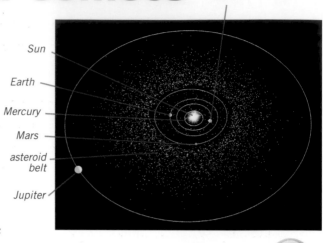

Venus
Sun
Earth
Mercury
Mars
asteroid belt
Jupiter

Most asteroids are further from the Sun than our own planet.

**DID YOU KNOW?**

The largest asteroid, Ceres, is 975 kilometres (605 miles) across.

## Parts of a comet

When a comet is warmed by the Sun, a large cloud of gas and dust is produced. The cloud can be a million kilometres across. The Sun pushes the cloud out behind the comet and forms two tails. The tails can grow to be hundreds of millions of kilometres long.

Comets have two tails. The white tail is made of dust. The blue tail is made of gas.

## BIOGRAPHY

### Edmond Halley
Edmond Halley (1656–1742) was the first person to work out the path of a comet and predict when it would be seen again (every 76 years). Halley's Comet was named in his honour although he did not discover it. Records show that Halley's Comet has been observed for more than 2,000 years.

# Satellites

Satellites orbit (travel around) our planet. Man-made satellites are machines travelling hundreds of kilometres above our heads.

Satellites carry all kinds of equipment, such as measuring instruments, telescopes, cameras, and radios. The radios send information and pictures back to Earth.

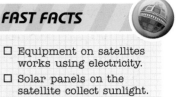

**FAST FACTS**

☐ Equipment on satellites works using electricity.
☐ Solar panels on the satellite collect sunlight.
☐ The solar panels make electricity for the satellite.

## What are satellites like?

Satellites are built from light but strong materials. They come in many shapes and sizes. For example, the scientific satellite Lageos is a sphere about the size of a beach ball. However, the Hubble Space Telescope is more than 13 metres (43 feet) long and weighs 11 tonnes (12 tons).

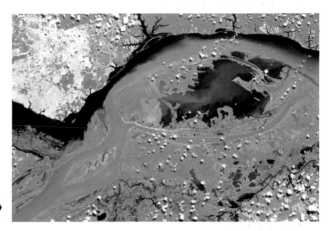

This photo was taken by a satellite. It shows the River Amazon running through the rainforest in Brazil. ⬢

## Types of satellite

- Communications satellites pass on all kinds of signals. These signals include television programmes, telephone calls, and e-mail messages.

- Weather satellites take pictures of clouds and measure conditions in the air. Some satellites take pictures of the Earth's surface. These pictures show up details that cannot be seen in ordinary photographs.

- Astronomy satellites carry telescopes into space, where they can see more clearly. Navigation satellites help ships to travel across the oceans and aircraft to find their way in the sky.

**DID YOU KNOW?**

*If you threw a ball into the air at 28,000 kilometres (17,400 miles) per hour, it would never fall down. It would become a satellite of the Earth.*

◀ This satellite is orbiting Earth.

# Moon

The Moon is the Earth's natural satellite. A satellite is something that travels around a planet.

The Moon is a ball of rock. There is no life on the Moon and hardly anything has changed there for millions of years.

## FAST FACTS

**Moon data**
- ☐ Diameter: 3,476 km (2,160 miles)
- ☐ Average distance from Earth: 384,400 km (238,900 miles)
- ☐ Time taken to orbit the Earth: 27.33 days
- ☐ Time taken to spin on its axis (line between the poles): 27.33 days
- ☐ Time between new Moons: 29.53 days

This vehicle is a lunar rover. The lunar rover was used on Moon missions to explore large areas.

## Landing on the Moon

Neil Armstrong and Buzz Aldrin were the first people to land on the Moon. They arrived there on 20 July 1969. The soil was grey and crunchy under their feet. The Sun shone from a completely black sky.

When astronauts visit the Moon, they collect rock samples and carry out experiments.

## Craters everywhere

The Moon is covered with craters. Rocks crashed down from space and caused the craters. They range from a few centimetres wide to 295 kilometres (183 miles) wide.

The flat, dark areas between the craters are called seas. But they are dry, rocky land.

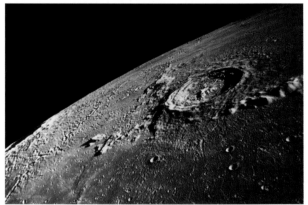

## The Moon's phases

The Sun shines on the Moon. On the part of the Moon facing the Sun, it is daytime. The other half is in darkness and here it is night. As the Moon orbits the Earth, we see different amounts of its sunlit half. The shape of the Moon is called its phase.

last quarter

new Moon

Earth

full Moon

first quarter

The Moon as seen from space (above) and from the Earth (below).

new Moon      first quarter      full Moon      last quarter

# Stars and galaxies

Every star is a giant ball of hot, glowing gas. Our Sun is a star. It looks different from the other stars in the sky because it is much closer to us.

Galaxies are enormous families of stars. The Sun belongs to our own galaxy, the Milky Way. Billions of galaxies are scattered through the universe.

## A star's life

Stars do not last forever. They are born and they die. Our Sun is about 5,000 million years old now. In another 5,000 million years, it will swell and become a red giant. Its outer layers will blow away. Eventually it will completely fade away.

Bigger stars swell and become red supergiants. Then they explode! These massive explosions are called supernovae.

▼ Different types of star have different life cycles. The lives of a large and small star are shown here.

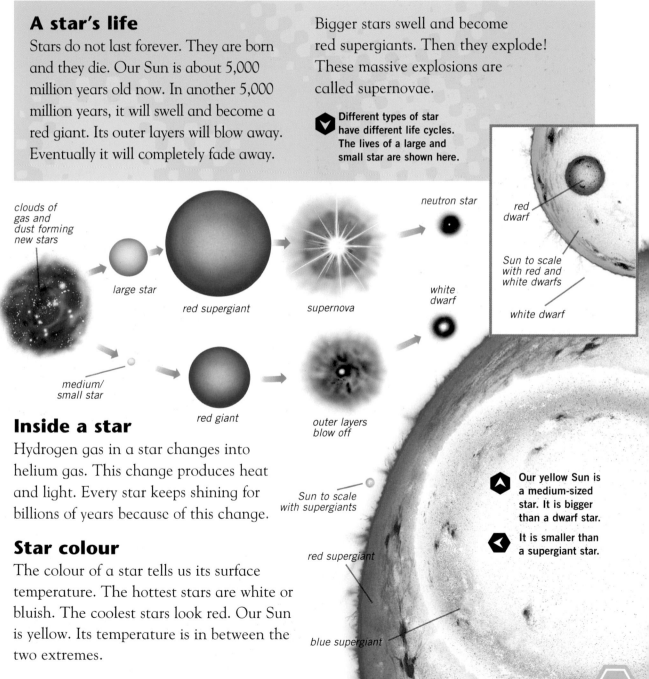

clouds of gas and dust forming new stars

large star

red supergiant

supernova

neutron star

medium/small star

red giant

outer layers blow off

white dwarf

red dwarf

Sun to scale with red and white dwarfs

white dwarf

Sun to scale with supergiants

red supergiant

blue supergiant

▲ Our yellow Sun is a medium-sized star. It is bigger than a dwarf star.

◄ It is smaller than a supergiant star.

## Inside a star

Hydrogen gas in a star changes into helium gas. This change produces heat and light. Every star keeps shining for billions of years because of this change.

## Star colour

The colour of a star tells us its surface temperature. The hottest stars are white or bluish. The coolest stars look red. Our Sun is yellow. Its temperature is in between the two extremes.

## Galaxy shapes

The Milky Way is a spiral galaxy. It has arms that spiral out from the centre. Most galaxies are the shape of a squashed ball. They are called elliptical galaxies. Some galaxies do not have a definite shape. They are called irregular galaxies.

 A spiral galaxy.

The Large Magellanic Cloud is a small irregular galaxy.

## Galaxy sizes

A light year is the distance that light travels in a year. Light travels through space at about 300,000 kilometres (186,000 miles) per second. One light year is an unimaginably long distance.

Dwarf galaxies are about 2,000 light years across. Giant galaxies contain millons of stars and are more than 500,000 light years across.

## Crashing galaxies

Galaxies are always moving through space. Sometimes, two galaxies crash into each other. Their shapes change and new stars form.

 These two galaxies are colliding.

# Universe

The universe is everything that exists. Scientists think that the universe contains more than 100,000 million galaxies.

The universe may have formed in a huge explosion called the 'Big Bang'.

## The formation of the universe

Scientists think that the Big Bang happened about 15,000 million years ago. At the beginning, the universe was unimaginably hot. The universe expanded and started to cool down.

After about one billion years, the first stars and galaxies formed. Planets formed around some of the stars. The universe carried on expanding. It is still expanding today.

A view of lots of galaxies in deep space, taken from the Hubble Space Telescope.

## Looking at the universe

The Hubble Space Telescope orbits the Earth. It points out into space. It has revealed many galaxies that are between 12,000 million and 14,000 million light years away!

The scale of the universe. Each of these pictures shows a much larger area than the previous one.

1. *the Solar System* about 0.1 light year across

2. *the Milky Way* about 100,000 light years across

3. *the universe* more than 14,000 million light years across

# Space travel

The Space Age began in 1957. Russia launched a spacecraft called Sputnik 1. It went into orbit around the Earth.

Since then, humans have been into space, and robot spacecraft have travelled towards the edge of our Solar System.

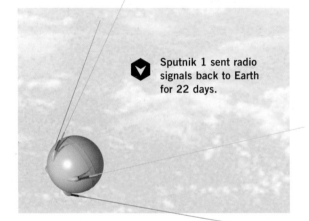

Sputnik 1 sent radio signals back to Earth for 22 days.

This rocket carried Yuri Gagarin into space.

## Early spacecraft

The first objects launched were satellites. These are spacecraft that circle round and round the Earth in orbit.

Soon after Sputnik 1 was launched, Russia sent Sputnik 2 into space. It carried the first ever space traveller – a dog called Laika.

## First human in space

In April 1961, Russian pilot Yuri Gagarin became the fastest man alive and the first man in space. He was sent into space at a speed of nearly 8 kilometres (5 miles) per second. He said afterwards, 'The rocket engines were creating the music of the future.'

## Moon visits

In 1968, humans flew around the Moon for the first time. Their spacecraft was called Apollo 8.

In July 1969, Apollo 11 landed on the Moon. Since then, there have been five manned moon landings.

Buzz Aldrin walks on the Moon.

## Space probes

Space probes are robotic spacecraft. They do not carry people. Since the Moon landings, space probes have explored all the planets in the Solar System, except Pluto. They have visited many of the planets' moons as well.

Two probes, called Voyager 1 and Voyager 2, have reached the edge of the Solar System. They have been travelling for over 30 years, and are now heading for the stars.

## Space stations

The International Space Station (ISS) is a spacecraft in which people can live for months at a time. The ISS orbits the Earth at 27,750 kilometres (17,240 miles) per hour. It is still being built and should be completed by 2010.

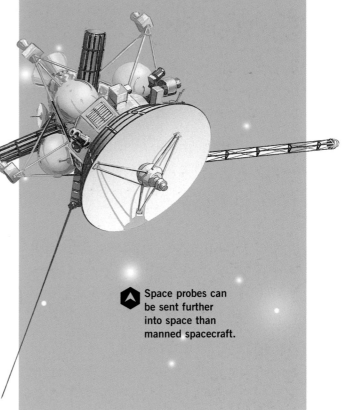

Space probes can be sent further into space than manned spacecraft.

Astronauts living in the International Space Station.

### Key dates

- ☐ 1957 Sputnik 1 and 2 are launched into orbit.
- ☐ 1961 Yuri Gagarin is the first man in space.
- ☐ 1963 Valentina Tereshkova is the first woman in space.
- ☐ 1969 Neil Armstrong and Buzz Aldrin walk on the Moon.
- ☐ 1977 Voyager 1 and 2 are launched into space.
- ☐ 1998 The first part of the ISS is launched.
- ☐ 2000 Astronauts live in the ISS for the first time.
- ☐ 2007 The Phoenix space probe is sent to Mars.

# Energy

Every action needs energy to make it happen. You need energy to run, jump, and shout. Machines need energy to work.

Energy comes in many forms. Light, heat, sound, and electricity are all forms of energy.

## Energy from the Sun

Energy from the Sun keeps all living things alive. As plants grow, they store the Sun's energy in their body parts. We eat plants. We also eat plant-eating animals. All the energy in our food comes from plants.

## Changing energy

Energy can change from one form to another. A television takes electrical energy from a power point. It changes it into light and sound energy as the programme appears on the screen.

### BIOGRAPHY

**James Prescott Joule**
A joule is a unit that scientists use to measure energy. It is named after the British scientist James Prescott Joule (1818–1889). He realized that energy cannot be destroyed, but it can change its form. Many foods have their energy value printed on the packet. It is in kilojoules (kJ), or thousands of joules.

Fuels store a lot of energy. The energy in fuel changes to movement energy in this dragster car.

Most of our energy comes through space from the Sun in the form of heat and light. The energy changes its form as it is used.

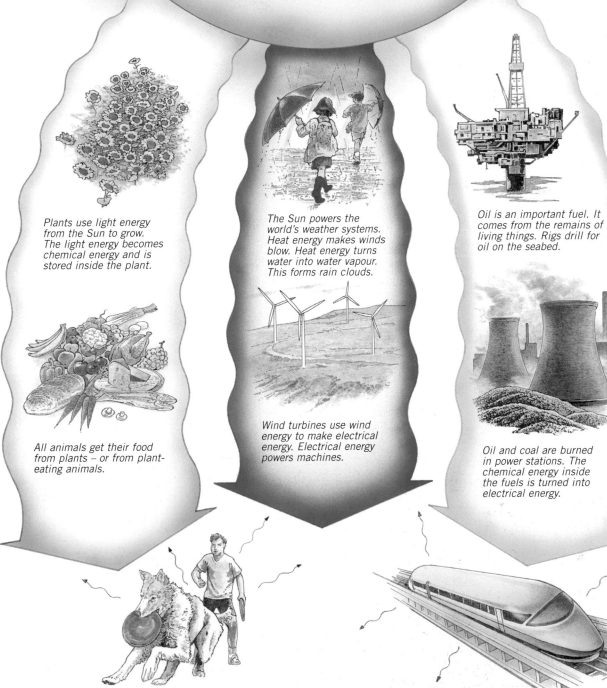

Plants use light energy from the Sun to grow. The light energy becomes chemical energy and is stored inside the plant.

All animals get their food from plants – or from plant-eating animals.

The Sun powers the world's weather systems. Heat energy makes winds blow. Heat energy turns water into water vapour. This forms rain clouds.

Wind turbines use wind energy to make electrical energy. Electrical energy powers machines.

Oil is an important fuel. It comes from the remains of living things. Rigs drill for oil on the seabed.

Oil and coal are burned in power stations. The chemical energy inside the fuels is turned into electrical energy.

The chemical energy in food allows people and animals to move and play. Their bodies change the chemical energy into movement energy.

Electrical energy powers machines such as high-speed trains. The electrical energy changes into movement energy as the train moves along the track.

# Heat and temperature

Heat is a form of energy. Objects with a lot of heat energy feel warm or hot. Objects with less heat energy feel cool or cold.

Temperature is a measure of how hot or cold something is.

Making toast uses heat. Too much heat causes the toast to burn.

## Heating and cooling

Everything is made of tiny particles called atoms and molecules. These particles are always moving. When heat energy flows into a substance, the extra energy makes the particles move faster. When heat is lost from a substance, the particles slow down.

## How heat flows

Heat flows in three ways:

- Conduction – Heat from a gas flame enters the base of a saucepan. It flows through the metal and into the water in the pan.

- Convection – Hot water rises from the base of the pan. When it gets to the top, it sinks. The cycle continues and the water is heated.

- Radiation – In a toaster, red-hot wires give out heat rays. They travel through the air to the bread. This kind of heat flow is called radiation.

## Bigger and smaller

Heat energy also makes a substance's particles move apart. This is why a heated substance expands (gets bigger). When it gets colder and the particles slow down, they also move closer together. The substance contracts (gets smaller).

Most materials contract when they freeze. Water is different. It expands as it turns to ice. This makes ice less dense, so it floats in water, like this iceberg.

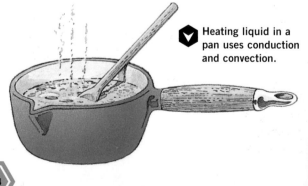

Heating liquid in a pan uses conduction and convection.

## Temperature scales

The Celsius scale measures temperature in degrees Celsius (°C). Ice has a temperature of 0°C, your body temperature is 37°C, and boiling water is 100°C.

The Fahrenheit scale measures temperature in degrees Fahrenheit (°F). Ice has a temperature of 32°F, your body temperature is 98°F, and boiling water is 212°F.

## Thermometers

Thermometers measure temperature. A glass thermometer contains a liquid inside a thin tube. It rises when it is warmed and drops when cooled. The temperature is read off the scale along the thermometer.

A digital thermometer has a screen that displays the number of degrees.

## Thermostats

A heating system warms the rooms of a house. Thermostats control the temperature. The thermostat switches the heating on if the room is too cool. It switches the heating off when it gets too hot.

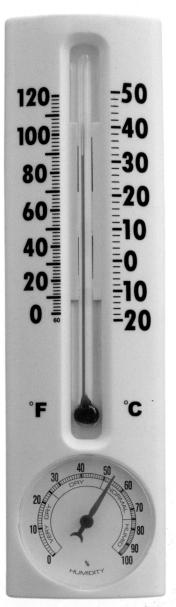

◄ The coloured liquid in this thermometer is alcohol.

**DID YOU KNOW?**

When you shiver, your muscles create heat. This makes you warmer. Sweating cools you down. It stops your body from overheating.

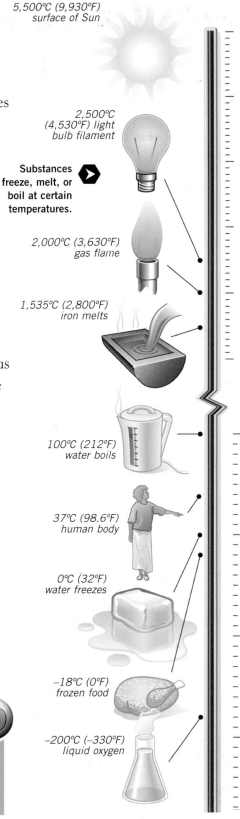

5,500°C (9,930°F) surface of Sun

2,500°C (4,530°F) light bulb filament

**Substances freeze, melt, or boil at certain temperatures.** ▶

2,000°C (3,630°F) gas flame

1,535°C (2,800°F) iron melts

100°C (212°F) water boils

37°C (98.6°F) human body

0°C (32°F) water freezes

−18°C (0°F) frozen food

−200°C (−330°F) liquid oxygen

# Conductors and insulators

Conductors are materials that let electricity or heat flow through them. Insulators are materials that do not let electricity or heat flow through them. We use conductors and insulators in our everyday lives without even realizing.

## Metal conductors

Metals are good conductors of heat and electricity. The ring of an electric stove glows red-hot when electricity travels through it. Saucepans are made of metal. They conduct heat from the stove to the food inside them.

Metal rings heat up very quickly because they are good heat conductors.

A polar bear's hairs are hollow. The air inside the hairs insulates the bear and keeps it warm.

## Heat insulators

Saucepans have handles made of plastic or wood. Heat cannot travel through plastic or wood. They are insulators. The handle stays cool, even if the pan is very hot.

## Insulation in nature

Animals that live in cold places use insulation to keep them warm. Fur and feathers trap a layer of air around the animal's body. The air insulates the animal – it keeps warmth in and keeps cold out.

## Electrical wires

The electrical wires in your home are made of copper. Copper is very good at conducting electricity. The copper is coated with plastic. Plastic is a good electrical insulator. It stops the electricity leaving the wire.

These ceramic (pottery) discs are insulators. They are placed between power lines and the pylons that hold them up. The discs stop electricity from flowing into the pylon.

ceramic discs

# Forces

A force is a push or a pull. You use a pushing force when you kick a ball. You use a pulling force to stop a lively dog on a lead.

Forces make moving things speed up, slow down, stop, change direction, or change shape.

## Speeding up and slowing down

When you pedal your bike, you exert a pushing force on the pedals. This force moves the bike along. The harder you pedal, the more force you apply, and the faster you move.

Magnetic force between a magnet and steel paper clips allows the magnet to pick up the paper clips.

To stop, you squeeze the brakes. The brake pads squeeze the wheel. Friction between the brake pads and the wheel stops the wheel moving.

## Forces on still objects

Forces do not disappear when objects stay still. All the parts of a building – the floors, walls, and beams – push or pull on each other. These forces exactly balance. If they did not balance, the whole structure might collapse.

◄ This baseball player exerts a pushing force when he throws the ball.

## Stretch, bend, and break

When forces try to move a fixed object, the object changes shape. It may get smaller or bigger, bend, twist, or even snap.

Over many years, the force of the wind blowing on the tree has made the tree bend. ►

# Floating and sinking

Wood, boats, air-filled balloons, and empty bottles float in water.
Stones, marbles, and bottles full of liquid do not float in water. But why?

## How objects float

When an empty bottle enters the water,
it displaces (pushes aside) the water.
The weight of the displaced water
pushes back on the bottle. The water
forces the bottle upwards and it floats.

Anyone can float in the Dead Sea. The
water there is very salty. It has more upward
force than fresh water or ordinary seawater.

BIOGRAPHY

**Archimedes**
The ancient Greek scientist
Archimedes once got into a full
bath and made it overflow. He
realized that putting an object
in water was a simple way to
measure its volume. The amount
of water that overflowed was
the same as his volume. This
discovery led him to explain
why things float.

## To sink, or not to sink

If an object is too heavy, the weight of
the displaced water cannot push hard
enough. The object will sink. This is
why heavy stones and bricks sink.

Heavy objects can float if they are
hollow. Boats float as long as they do
not carry too many people or goods that
are too heavy.

Hollow objects float. If
this bottle was filled with
water, it would sink.

# Friction

Friction is a force that stops one material sliding over another. There is friction between a car's tyres and the road. When the car travels around a corner, the friction stops the car from sliding right across the road.

## Using friction

Friction is also needed for a vehicle to move in the first place. Friction allows the wheels to grip the ground and this helps to push the vehicle forwards.

Objects that are held together by screws would fall apart without friction. Friction helps the screw grip the wood around it.

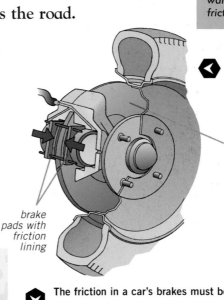

Cars brake pads grip a disc attached to the wheel. This produces friction to slow the car down.

brake disc, rotating with wheel

brake pads with friction lining

## Smooth surfaces

A smooth surface has very little friction. Ice is very smooth. You slip on ice because there is not enough friction between your shoes and the ice.

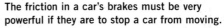

The friction in a car's brakes must be very powerful if they are to stop a car from moving.

The bottom of skis are very smooth. The skier travels very fast.

## Reducing friction

Friction is not always useful. Machines have moving parts. If there is too much friction, the parts will heat up and the machine may become damaged. Oil or grease is added to make the moving parts slippery. This is called lubrication. It reduces friction.

# Gravity

When you throw a ball up into the air, it will fall back down. A force called gravity pulls everything towards the ground.

Both balls take exactly the same time to reach the ground. This is because both balls fall from the same height.

## The Earth's gravity

Whenever two objects are near each other, gravity tries to pull them together. The more mass (amount of material) in both objects, the stronger the force of gravity.

The Earth has a large mass. This is why there is a strong force of gravity between the Earth and everything that is on or near it.

An astronaut floats in space above the Earth. Gravity causes the astronaut to move in an orbit around the Earth.

**DID YOU KNOW?**

The Earth's force of gravity extends out into space. Gravity keeps the Moon in its orbit (path) around the Earth.

## Gaining and losing weight

The force of gravity between you and the Earth pulls you down. Your weight is the amount of force that you exert on the ground – or on weighing scales.

If you flew to the Moon, you would weigh only a sixth of your Earth weight. This is because the Moon is much smaller than the Earth. It has only about one-sixth of the Earth's gravity.

# Motion

To make an object move, a force must push or pull it. Once the object is moving, it carries on by itself. It will keep going until another force makes it stop.

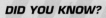

## Starting and stopping

A ball moves when it is thrown into the air. It rises into the air until gravity pulls it back down to Earth.

A ball moves when it is rolled along the ground. It rolls until friction slows it down.

A bike moves when you pedal. It stops when you brake.

## Turning

A moving object will not change direction unless a force acts on it. When you are rolling along on your bike, you pull the handlebars to change direction.

When you ride on a bicycle, you speed up, turn, slow down, and stop.

push off and pedal to start moving

travel at a steady speed pedalling on flat ground

speed up as gravity pulls you downhill

pedal harder going uphill to overcome gravity

turn the handlebars to change direction

pull on the brakes to stop

When skydivers first leap from an aircraft, they accelerate (speed up).

## More weight, less speed

Have you ever seen people push a car to get it moving? Even though the car can roll easily, it takes a lot of force to get it moving. This is because the car is very heavy. The more it is pushed, the faster it goes.

# Light

Light is a type of energy. The Sun gives off light. Burning sticks, hot coals, and light bulbs also give off light.

Without light, you could not see. You can only see things that give out light or reflect (bounce) light into your eyes.

## Speed of light

When you switch on a torch, you don't have to wait for it to light something up. This is because light travels extremely quickly.

Light from the Sun travels across space to the Earth. It takes 8 minutes to make this journey, which is 150 million kilometres (93 million miles).

## Absorbing light

Light travels in straight lines. When light hits an object, some of the light energy is absorbed (taken in). Dark, rough objects absorb most of the light that hits them.

You can see straight beams of light when mist is in the air, like in this forest.

## Reflecting light

Objects reflect light as well as absorb it. Shiny, smooth objects reflect light very well. They reflect light rays in the same direction. This is why you can see yourself in a shiny, clean window or mirror.

Uneven surfaces, such as paper, cloth, or wood, reflect light in all directions. They do not look shiny.

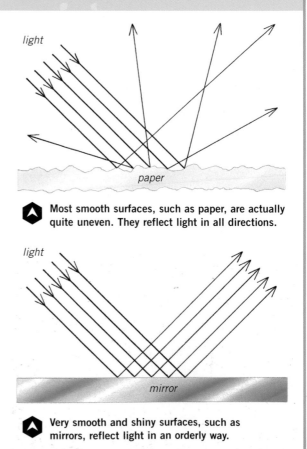

Most smooth surfaces, such as paper, are actually quite uneven. They reflect light in all directions.

Very smooth and shiny surfaces, such as mirrors, reflect light in an orderly way.

## Transparent and opaque

Some objects allow light to travel right through them. These objects are transparent (see-through). Glass and water are transparent. Other objects do not let any light pass through them. They are opaque.

Water is transparent, but when it is very still it acts like a mirror. You can see the mountain reflected in the lake. ▶

## Sight

Your eyes collect light. Special cells inside the eye detect the light and send signals to the brain. The brain turns these signals into pictures.

## Refraction

Light travels more slowly in glass or water than in air. When light rays enter a transparent object, they bend. This is called refraction.

If you put a stick in a glass of water, the stick looks bent. Light coming from the end of the stick is bent by the water.

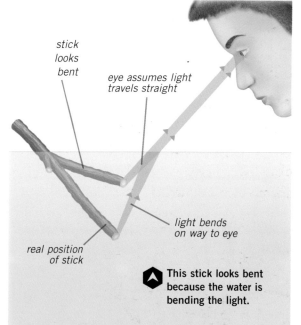

*stick looks bent*

*eye assumes light travels straight*

*light bends on way to eye*

*real position of stick*

This stick looks bent because the water is bending the light.

## Measuring distance

In space, light travels 9,461 million million kilometres (5,880 million million miles) in a year. Astronomers call this distance a light year. They use it to measure the distances to stars and galaxies.

◀ Light from the Trifid Nebula takes about 4,500 light years to reach the Earth.

# Colour

White light is really a mixture of different colours. When you see a rainbow, you are seeing white light split into its colours.

Objects look coloured depending on which coloured lights they reflect.

## Spectrum of colours

A prism is a see-through block that is pyramid shaped. When light is shone on to a prism, it separates the colours in white light. The pattern of colours that you see is called a spectrum.

Tiny water droplets in the air split sunlight into the spectrum of colours.

## Primary colours of light

The primary colours of light are red, green, and blue. It is possible to make any other colour by mixing different amounts of these three colours.

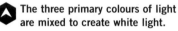 The three primary colours of light are mixed to create white light.

## Coloured objects

Most of the objects we see reflect light to our eyes. A snowman reflects all the colours of light. It looks white. A tarmac road hardly reflects any light. It looks black.

Some objects reflect only some of the colours of light. A red car reflects red light. It absorbs (soaks up) the other colours of the spectrum.

## Primary colours of pigments

The primary colours of pigments such as paints are red, blue, and yellow. You can mix them to make all other colours except white.

The three primary colours of pigments mix together to make black.

# Sound and music

Sounds can be loud or quiet, high or low. Sounds allow us to talk to each other and sounds tell us about our surroundings.

Music is a collection of sounds that have been arranged to sound interesting. Music can make you happy, sad, relaxed, or excited.

## Vibrations

When someone strums a guitar, you hear a sound. Strumming makes the guitar's strings vibrate (shake) very quickly. The air carries these sound vibrations into your ear. Your brain makes sense of the sounds.

## High and low

A whistle makes a very high-pitched sound. Its vibrations are very fast. A bass guitar makes a very low-pitched sound. Its vibrations are much slower.

The frequency of a sound is the number of vibrations made in one second. High-pitched sounds have a high frequency. Low-pitched sounds have a low frequency.

### DID YOU KNOW?

Hummingbirds hover by flapping their wings very quickly. Their wings shake the air as they move. The result is a beautiful humming sound.

An ambulance makes a high-pitched wailing sound.

## Loud and quiet

Loud sounds are made by big vibrations. A big truck driving past makes big vibrations. Quiet sounds are made by small vibrations. A field mouse rustling through grass makes small vibrations.

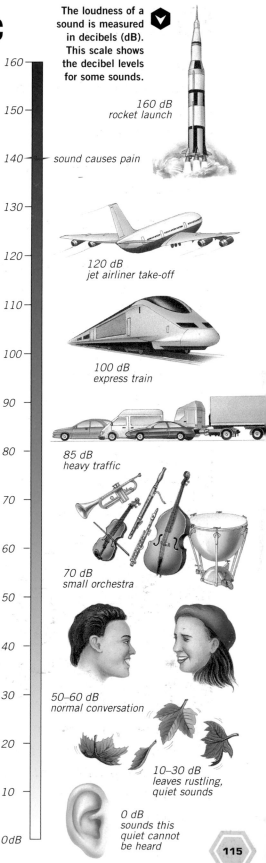

The loudness of a sound is measured in decibels (dB). This scale shows the decibel levels for some sounds.

160 —
150 —
140 —
130 —
120 —
110 —
100 —
90 —
80 —
70 —
60 —
50 —
40 —
30 —
20 —
10 —
0dB

160 dB
rocket launch

sound causes pain

120 dB
jet airliner take-off

100 dB
express train

85 dB
heavy traffic

70 dB
small orchestra

50–60 dB
normal conversation

10–30 dB
leaves rustling, quiet sounds

0 dB
sounds this quiet cannot be heard

**115**

## Musical notes

In music, sounds are organized into notes. Every note has a certain pitch. A scale is a sequence of notes.

A harmony is when two or more notes with different pitches are sounded together. The length of a note can change. The mix of long and short sounds adds rhythm. Rhythm is very important in most music.

## Singers

The human voice is a simple musical instrument. It can make beautiful music. Our vocal cords are tiny strings in our throat. Air passes over them when we breathe in and out and it makes them vibrate. This creates sound. To change the note that we sing, we tighten and relax the vocal cords and throat.

 A singer's voice is made louder by a microphone.

## Musical instruments

All musical instruments make vibrations. The vibrations produce musical notes. There are three main types of instrument. String instruments make notes from vibrating strings. Wind instruments have to be blown. Percussion instruments have to be struck.

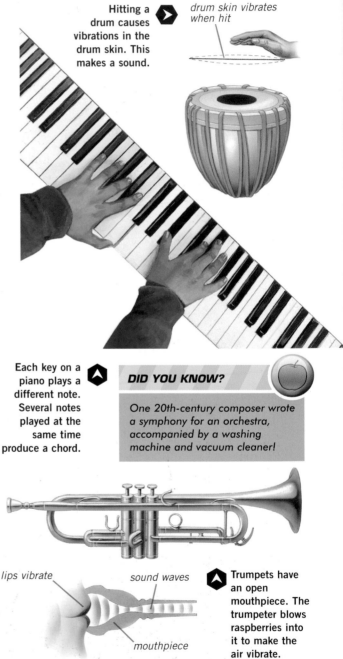

Hitting a drum causes vibrations in the drum skin. This makes a sound.

drum skin vibrates when hit

Each key on a piano plays a different note. Several notes played at the same time produce a chord.

**DID YOU KNOW?**

One 20th-century composer wrote a symphony for an orchestra, accompanied by a washing machine and vacuum cleaner!

lips vibrate

sound waves

mouthpiece

Trumpets have an open mouthpiece. The trumpeter blows raspberries into it to make the air vibrate.

# Electricity and circuits

Electricity is a very useful type of energy. It powers trains, computers, lights, televisions, and many other types of machine.

A circuit is a path around which electricity can flow. Electric circuits are everywhere – inside machines, homes, cars, and offices.

## What is electricity?

All substances are made of tiny particles called atoms. In the middle of each atom there is a core called a nucleus. Around the nucleus are particles called electrons. Electricity is the movement of electrons.

## Static electricity

Electrons can be rubbed off one material on to another. When you rub a balloon on your hair, electrons in your hair move to the balloon. An electric charge builds up on the balloon. This is called static electricity.

 The electric charge on a balloon can make your hair stand on end.

**DID YOU KNOW?**

The nerves in your brain send messages to each other in the form of bursts of electricity.

## Lightning

During a storm, static electricity builds up in thunderclouds. When enough static electricity has built up, the electricity jumps to the ground or to another cloud. This is lightning.

The lightning heats the air very suddenly. The air quickly expands (gets bigger). This produces a loud bang, which we call thunder.

◄ Metal rods called lightning conductors are put high on buildings. They make lightning strikes travel safely into the ground.

## Current electricity

When electrons flow along a wire, they make current electricity. Batteries or mains electricity push the electrons through the wire. Mains electricity is made in power stations. Current electricity can power a light bulb, turn a motor, and do many other useful jobs.

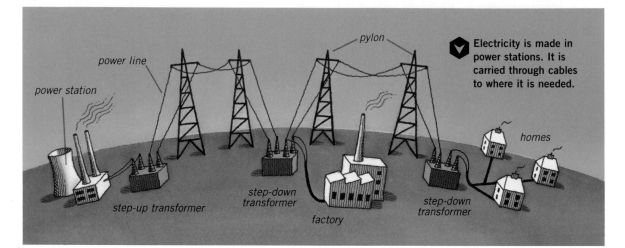

Electricity is made in power stations. It is carried through cables to where it is needed.

power line

power station

pylon

homes

step-up transformer

step-down transformer

factory

step-down transformer

## Circuits

For electricity to flow, it needs a complete path or loop around which to travel. This path is called an electric circuit. A torch contains a simple electric circuit.

## Switches

In any circuit, a switch can turn the electricity on or off. A switch completes a circuit to make electricity flow, and breaks the circuit to make electricity stop flowing.

In a torch, turning the switch on lets electricity travel and the bulb lights up.

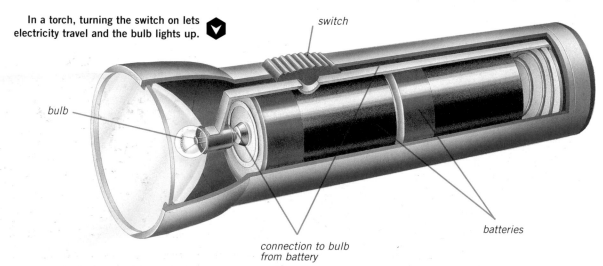

switch

bulb

connection to bulb from battery

batteries

# Magnetism

Magnetism is a force that is found in nature. Humans have known about magnetism for thousands of years.

A magnet can attract (pull towards) or repel (push away) other magnets. Huge magnets are used in power stations to make electricity.

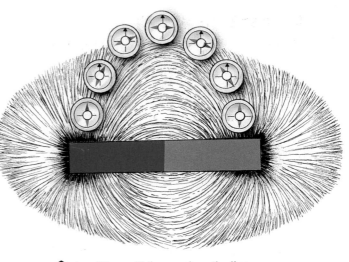

 Iron filings will line up along the lines of magnetic force around a magnet. A compass needle will point along the lines.

## Magnetic fields

All magnets are surrounded by an invisible magnetic field. This is an area where the magnetism can be felt. The field is strongest at the north and south poles of the magnet. On a bar-shaped magnet, the poles are at either end.

Magnets can only attract other magnetic materials, such as iron.

## Electromagnets

Electromagnets are very powerful types of magnet that can be switched on and off. They are made by passing an electric current through a coil of wire. Electromagnets are used in motors and doorbells.

## Magnets and navigation

Compass needles are magnetic. They always point to the north. This is because the Earth itself has a magnetic field. One magnetic pole is near the Earth's North Pole, and the other is near the South Pole. The compass needle lines up along Earth's magnetic field.

A compass helps us find our way from one place to the next.

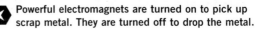 Powerful electromagnets are turned on to pick up scrap metal. They are turned off to drop the metal.

# Measurement

How big is that insect? How heavy is that rock? How hot is molten steel? These are questions that scientists need to answer when they carry out their work. Measurement helps them find their answers.

The flight deck of a space shuttle measures many things such as temperature, fuel levels, and speed.

## Units of measurement

To compare one set of measurements with another, it helps to use the same type of unit. In science, people use the metre to measure length and the second to measure time. They use the kilogram to measure mass (the amount of material in an object).

Most other units of measurement are based on these basic units. For example, speed is measured in metres per second.

## SI system

In the 1790s, the French began the invention of the SI system of measurement. This is sometimes called the metric system. Metres and seconds are two of the units of this system.

Most countries use the SI system. A few countries, including the United States, still use the old system. This is called the English, or Imperial, system. It uses measures such as the pound, foot, and inch.

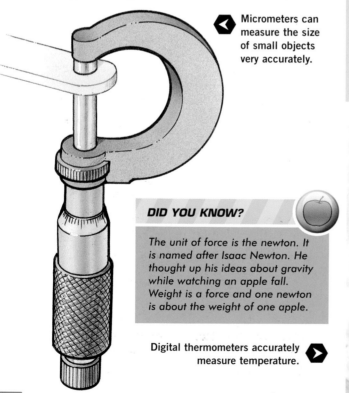

Micrometers can measure the size of small objects very accurately.

### DID YOU KNOW?

The unit of force is the newton. It is named after Isaac Newton. He thought up his ideas about gravity while watching an apple fall. Weight is a force and one newton is about the weight of one apple.

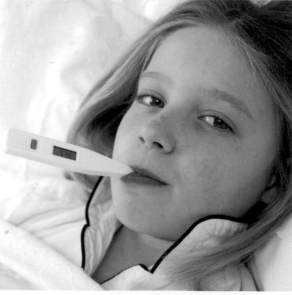

Digital thermometers accurately measure temperature.

# Mathematics

We use numbers and mathematics in our everyday lives. We first learn mathematics when we learn to count and to calculate with numbers. We count the number of children in a class, and we work out how many minutes until lunchtime.

## Numbers

The position of each digit in a number affects its meaning. In the number 3,512, the 3 stands for three thousand, the 5 stands for five hundred, the 1 stands for one ten, and the 2 stands for two ones.

## Probability

Probability is a way of working out the chance of something happening or not. When you toss a coin, it can either land on heads or tails. You will get one of the two possible outcomes – either heads or tails. So the probability is 1/2.

 Computers have made it possible to speed up mathematical calculations. This supercomputer can carry out 10 billion instructions every second.

## Arithmetic

In arithmetic, you can add (+), subtract (–), multiply (x), or divide (÷) numbers.

In addition and multiplication, the order of the numbers in a sum does not matter:

| | |
|---|---|
| 2 + 3 = 5 <br> **gives the same answer as** <br> 3 + 2 = 5 | 3 x 4 = 12 <br> **gives the same answer as** <br> 4 x 3 = 12 |

In subtraction and division, the order of the numbers in a sum is important:

| | |
|---|---|
| 4 – 1 = 3 <br> **does not give the same answer as** <br> 1 – 4 = –3 | 10 ÷ 5 = 2 <br> **does not give the same answer as** <br> 5 ÷ 10 = 0.5 |

 From an early age you are taught how to use numbers to tell the time.

# Time

Time is a way of dividing up our lives into sections. Each day, week, month, and year is a period of time.

In ancient times, before clocks, the Sun helped humans to tell the time.

## Days

The Earth spins once each day. At noon each day, the Sun is at its highest point in the sky. From here it sinks and travels west until sunset. At dawn the Sun appears in the east, then moves up until it is noon again.

The period between one noon and the next is one day. Each day is divided into hours, minutes, and seconds.

## Years

The Earth travels around the Sun. One complete journey around the Sun takes 365.25 days. This period is one year.

The shadow on a sundial moves as the Sun appears to move across the sky. You can read the time from where the shadow is pointing.

### DID YOU KNOW?

The Sun does not actually move across the sky. It is the Earth that moves. It spins on its axis (line between the poles) once a day.

## Calendars

Calendars are ways of organizing time. They are based on a year of 365 days. A year is split into 12 months. Every fourth year is a leap year, which has 366 days. The extra day is added in February.

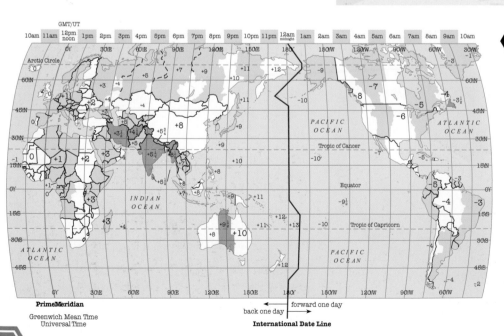

PrimeMeridian
Greenwich Mean Time
Universal Time

back one day → forward one day

**International Date Line**

Different places on the Earth have day and night at different times. The world is divided into 24 time 'zones'.

### Key

The numbers show how many hours ahead or behind Greenwich Mean Time (GMT) a place is. GMT is the time in London, UK.

- even number of hours different from GMT
- odd number of hours different from GMT
- ½-hour difference from adjacent zone
- less than ½-hour difference from adjacent zone

# Matter

Everything around us is made of matter. Rock, metal, water, air, wood, plastic, this book, and you are all made of matter.

Matter can exist as a solid, a liquid, and a gas. These are the three states of matter.

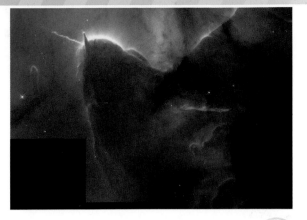

Using telescopes we can see some of the matter in the Universe – planets, stars, and clouds of gas like this nebula.

## Atoms

All matter is made up of tiny particles called atoms. Sometimes atoms join together to form bigger particles called molecules. Atoms and molecules are much too small to see without a microscope.

The three states of matter are solid, liquid, and gas.

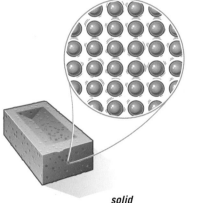

**solid**
*particles vibrate in their positions*

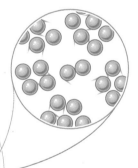

**liquid**
*particles move around more freely*

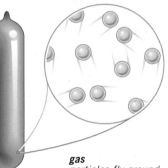

**gas**
*particles fly around completely freely*

## Mass and volume

Mass is a measure of how much matter is in an object. Mass is measured in kilograms or grams.

Matter takes up space – it has volume. Volume can be measured in cubic metres, cubic centimetres, or litres.

## Density

How much mass an object has for its size is called its density. High-density objects have a lot of mass for their volume. A stone on the beach has high density. Low-density objects do not have much mass for their volume. A hot-air balloon has low density.

# Solids

You can pick up solids. They do not flow through your fingers. ▶

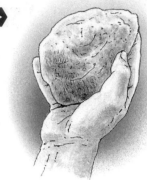

Most of the things we see around us are solids. Rocks, roads, books, pencils, computers, cars, skateboards, knives and forks are all solids.

Solids have definite shapes. You can pick up a solid object (as long as it's not too heavy!) and turn it around.

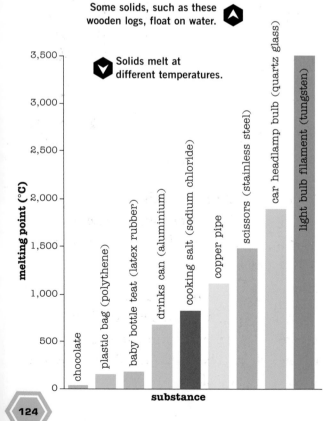

Some solids, such as these wooden logs, float on water. ⬆

Solids melt at different temperatures. ⬇

## Solids can be strong

The particles in a solid are held tightly together. This is why solids have shape and strength – unlike liquids or gases. If you tried to pick up some liquid or some gas, it would flow away between your fingers.

You can change the shape of some solids. You can bend, stretch, squash, or twist them. But it can be hard work. All solids try to keep their shapes.

## Melting solids

If you heat up a solid enough, the solid melts into a liquid. Different solids melt at different temperatures. Butter melts in your mouth, but iron only melts above 1,500°C (2,730°F).

### FAST FACTS

**Different types of solid**

☐ Table salt and diamond are solids called crystals. Their particles are arranged in a regular pattern.

☐ Rubber and glass are also solids but they are not crystals. Their particles are not arranged in a regular pattern. They are called amorphous (shapeless) solids.

# Liquids

Water is a liquid. Living things depend on water. There are also many other important liquids. Petrol is a liquid that is used as a fuel in cars.

Liquids do not have fixed shapes. They can flow, and take up the shape of whatever container they are in.

## Flowing liquids

The particles in a liquid are not held tightly together. They can move around. This is why liquids can flow.

Liquids aren't normally as strong as solids. You can easily push your hand through a still liquid. However, you cannot squeeze a liquid to make it take up less space.

**DID YOU KNOW?**

Liquids are not always soft. Very fine, high-pressure jets of water can slice through metal.

Some liquids are thicker than others. Thicker liquids like treacle flow more slowly than thinner liquids like water. If you drop a marble into different liquids, you will see that it falls more slowly through thicker liquids.

A pond skater can walk on the surface of a pond. The surface of a liquid behaves like a kind of skin. The pond skater is not heavy enough to break this 'skin'.

Liquid oil is poured into a car's engine. A funnel keeps the liquid flowing in the right direction.

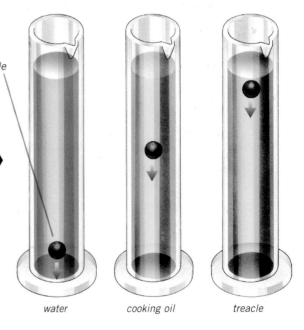

marble

water          cooking oil          treacle

## Cooling and heating

If you cool a liquid enough, it freezes into a solid. If you heat up a liquid enough, it boils and turns into a gas.

Many metal objects are made by first melting solid metal into a liquid. Then the liquid metal is poured into a mould. When the metal turns back into a solid, it takes the shape of the mould.

# Gases

You may think of gases as horrible, smelly substances. Some gases are like this, but not all are. The air is a mixture of gases. We cannot see or smell these gases.

Gases do not have fixed shapes. They flow easily and spread out to fill any container they are put in.

 Airships are filled with helium gas. Helium is lighter than air and this makes the airships float.

## Whizzing particles

The particles in a gas move around very fast. You can squeeze a gas to fit into a small container. If you put the same amount of gas into a larger container, it will expand (get bigger) to fill the new container.

## Heating and cooling gases

Liquids turn into gases when they are heated to boiling point. Water boils at 100°C (212°F). But many substances only turn into gases at very high temperatures. You need to heat molten iron to nearly 3,000°C (5,430°F) for it to boil.

When you cool a gas enough, it turns into a liquid (condenses). You can also turn a gas back into a liquid by squeezing it hard.

### DID YOU KNOW?

At room temperature, the particles in air travel at around 1,800 kilometres (1,120 miles) per hour – the same speed as a bullet fired from a rifle.

Gases from factories can pollute the air. Not all gases are like this.

## Pressure

Gas particles bounce around and hit each other. They also hit the walls of their container. This puts pressure on (pushes) the walls of the container. If you add more gas to the container, the pressure becomes greater.

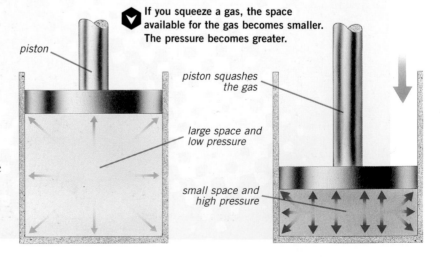

If you squeeze a gas, the space available for the gas becomes smaller. The pressure becomes greater.

piston

piston squashes the gas

large space and low pressure

small space and high pressure

# Mixtures and solutions

Sand is a mixture of tiny pieces of rocks and seashells. The air we breathe is a mixture of gases.

Seawater is a special kind of mixture called a solution. In a solution, one substance is dissolved in another substance. In the sea, salt is dissolved in water.

## Mixtures

In a mixture, the substances do not change. If you mix together talcum powder and tiny pieces of iron, there is no change in either substance. The iron filings are still magnetic. The talcum powder still soaks up water.

The sea is salty. After you have been in the sea, your skin will have salt left on it.

The substances in solutions can be solids, liquids, or gases. Fizzy drinks are solutions. They are fizzy because carbon dioxide gas is dissolved in the liquid.

The individual sweets in this mixture do not change.

## Filtering

You can pass some mixtures through a sieve or filter paper to separate them. Filter paper has tiny holes in it. The sieve or filter paper catches the large pieces and the small pieces go straight through.

To make 'real' coffee, hot water is mixed with coffee grains. Tiny holes in the filter paper let water through but not the large coffee grains.

coffee grains

filter paper

holes in the paper

liquid moves through

## Solutions

If you stir salt into water, the salt dissolves and makes a solution. You cannot see the salt anymore, but the water tastes salty.

# Water

Life on Earth would not exist without water. Plants and animals need water to survive. Two-thirds of your body is made of water. You need to drink up to 1.5 litres (3 pints) of water every day to stay healthy.

In hot countries, animals travel many miles to drink from water holes.

## What is water?

Water is made up of tiny particles called molecules. Each water molecule is made up of three even smaller particles called atoms. A water molecule has two atoms of hydrogen and one atom of oxygen.

## Properties of water

Scientists base the Celsius temperature scale on the freezing and boiling points of water. On this scale, water freezes into ice at 0°C (32°F) and boils into gas at 100°C (212°F).

Water can dissolve lots of different substances, such as sugar and salt. Chemists use water to make many things, from acids to medicines.

 Water exists as a gas (steam), a liquid (lake), and a solid (ice and snow).

## Hard and soft water

Some rivers pass over limestone rocks. The water dissolves chemicals from the rocks. The added chemicals make the water 'hard'. It is difficult to make a good lather with soap in hard water.

Soft water is water that does not contain chemicals from limestone rocks.

This water is soft water. It makes a good lather with soap.

# Oxygen

Oxygen is a gas. You cannot see it, smell it, or taste it. The air that you breathe contains oxygen. Oxygen is also part of the rocks that make up the Earth's surface.

## Uses of oxygen

Substances cannot burn unless oxygen is present. This is why oxygen is needed in making steel, plastics, explosives, and rocket fuels. It is even needed in treating sewage (liquid human waste).

In a fire, the burning material is actually combining (joining) with oxygen in the air.

## Oxygen and living things

Land animals breathe in oxygen from the air. Fish have gills so they can take oxygen from water.

Plants also need oxygen, but they produce more oxygen than they use. Oxygen is a waste product of photosynthesis. Photosynthesis is a process in which plants make their own sugary food.

High up in the atmosphere, the air is thinner and there is much less oxygen. Fighter pilots need to breathe from bottles of oxygen.

**DID YOU KNOW?**

Without plants to renew the oxygen supply in the air, we would soon run out of oxygen. The Amazon rainforest produces a fifth of all the oxygen made by plants.

## Ozone

Ozone is another kind of oxygen gas. It is poisonous, but there is normally only a very small amount in the air. Gases from car exhausts and sunlight react together. This can make extra ozone and cause breathing problems in some people.

However, ozone is important to us. High up in the Earth's atmosphere a thin layer of ozone protects us from harmful rays in sunlight.

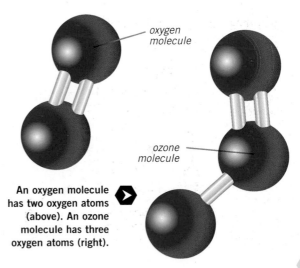

oxygen molecule

ozone molecule

An oxygen molecule has two oxygen atoms (above). An ozone molecule has three oxygen atoms (right).

# Detergents

Detergents are powerful cleaning chemicals. They can get rid of grease and dirt on dishes and clothes.

Detergents are made from chemicals in oil. Before people had detergents, they used soap for all types of cleaning.

## Beating the scum

When you use soap, it can form a messy scum. Detergents do not do this. They are also better at cleaning than soap.

Washing-up liquid, laundry detergents, and shampoos are all detergents. Laundry detergents contain brighteners to make clothes look extra bright. Shampoo contains ingredients to make your hair softer.

Detergents break up grease into pieces. Water washes the grease away.

## Detergents and birds

Oil can leak from a wrecked ship. Birds may become covered with oil. The only way to get the oil off is to use detergents. At bird sanctuaries, workers clean the birds and release them back into the wild.

This oil-covered bird has been caught and will be cleaned with detergent.

## How detergents work

Detergents are made up of lots of tiny molecules. The molecules have a head and a tail. The head 'likes' water. The tail 'likes' dirt.

The tails stick to the bits of dirt on clothes. Soon the dirt is surrounded. The heads 'stick' to the water. When the clothes move about, the water washes the dirt away.

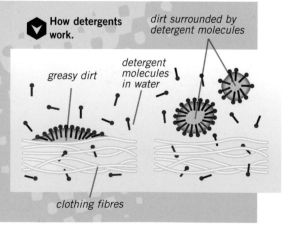

How detergents work.

dirt surrounded by detergent molecules

greasy dirt

detergent molecules in water

clothing fibres

# Dyes and pigments

Dyes are used to colour fabrics. Natural dyes come from plants and animals. Most dyes used today are synthetic (man-made).

Pigments are colouring substances used to colour inks and paints.

## Natural dyes

Saffron is a natural dye. It is obtained from crocus flowers. Other plant dyes include madder (red) and indigo (blue). These come from the madder and indigo plants. Cochineal red is a dye that comes from insects.

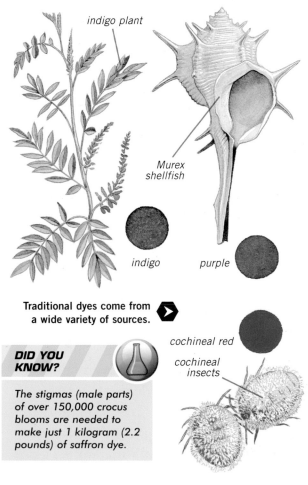

*indigo plant*

*Murex shellfish*

*indigo*     *purple*

Traditional dyes come from a wide variety of sources. ▶

*cochineal red*

*cochineal insects*

**DID YOU KNOW?**

The stigmas (male parts) of over 150,000 crocus blooms are needed to make just 1 kilogram (2.2 pounds) of saffron dye.

▲ Newly dyed cotton hangs out to dry in Rajasthan, India.

## Synthetic dyes

Synthetic dyes are usually made with chemicals from crude oil. Synthetic dyes have more brilliant colours than natural dyes. They do not wash out or fade as easily.

## Pigments

Dyes dissolve in water. Pigments do not dissolve in water. Traditional pigments include coloured earths such as ochre, and chemicals containing metals, such as iron oxide. Today, most pigments are synthetic.

# Petrol and diesel

The vehicles on our roads are powered by petrol or diesel. These chemicals come from crude oil. They are burned inside engines.

Petrol and diesel can also power many other machines, from lawnmowers and boats to trains and small aircraft.

## Inside a petrol engine

Petrol is burned in a petrol engine. In a car, the heat forces pistons up and down. This movement turns a crankshaft. The crankshaft drives the wheels.

Petrol engines in chainsaws must be small, light, and carry their own fuel.

## Diesel engines

Diesel is burned in a diesel engine. Diesel engines are simpler and tougher than petrol engines. They also do not use up as much fuel. However, they produce more pollution than a petrol engine.

Boats with petrol or diesel engines are very noisy.

We rely on diesel and petrol to fuel our cars. We need to find a new type of fuel. Oil on our planet is almost all used up.

## Chainsaws

Petrol engines are powerful. A chainsaw has a petrol engine. The chain has sharp teeth on it. When the engine is switched on, the chain rotates (turns). It can quickly cut through a thick trunk or a branch of a tree.

## Fumes

Both petrol and diesel engines produce waste gases. Some of the gases are made harmless before they leave the machine. But carbon dioxide is released into the air by both engines. Carbon dioxide is contributing to global warming.

# Reactions

Chemistry doesn't just happen in science laboratories. Chemical reactions are going on all around you. Rusting, burning, cooking, and breathing all involve chemical reactions.

Eggs change when they are heated. You cannot undo this change.

## Reactants and products

In a chemical reaction, two or more chemicals interact with each other. A change happens and new substances are produced.

Chemicals at the start of a reaction are called the reactants. Chemicals at the end of a reaction are called the products.

A chemical reaction inside fireflies produces light.

## Rusting

Iron is a strong, grey metal. Oxygen is an invisible gas. Iron reacts with oxygen in the air. The product is iron oxide – rust. Iron oxide is a reddish, crumbly solid.

## Cooking

Lots of different reactions go on in cooking. When you fry or boil an egg, the clear runny liquid hardens and turns white. A chemical reaction has taken place.

Firework displays involve very fast, explosive chemical reactions.

## Industry

Chemical reactions are very important in many industries. They are used to make a huge range of products, from fertilizers and explosives to cleaning fluids and dyes.

Some industries use living things as miniature chemical factories. Yeast is a type of fungus. It helps to make bread and beer.

# Fuels

Fuels are the most useful energy source we have. They contain a lot of energy. When they burn, they release their energy as heat and light.

Every time you switch on a lamp, use a heater, take a ride in a car, bus, train, or aeroplane, fuel is being burned.

## Fossil fuels

The main fuels are coal, crude oil, and natural gas. These are known as fossil fuels. Petrol and diesel for engines come from crude oil. Some heaters and cookers burn gas to make heat. Electricity comes from power stations that burn fuels such as coal and gas.

In hot countries, people may collect cow dung and then dry it in the Sun to produce a fuel.

## An energy-hungry world

We burn fuels in huge quantities. This produces smoke, fumes, and waste gases, including carbon dioxide. Extra carbon dioxide in the air is causing the world's temperatures to rise – global warming. To help stop global warming, we need to burn less fuel.

How fossil fuels form.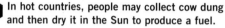

1. tiny sea creatures died and sank

2. layers of rock gradually built up and changed their remains into liquid oil and gas

3. oil and gas moved upwards

4. oil and gas collected underneath a rock layer

1. trees and plants decayed very slowly in swampy areas

2. rotting plants formed a layer of peat

3. peat was buried under layers of mud and sand

4. millions of years later hard layers of coal formed

## Nuclear fuel

Nuclear fuel produces huge amounts of heat energy. It is used in nuclear power stations to generate electricity. Nuclear waste is dangerous. It must be disposed of carefully.

# Fire

Humans first learnt how to use fire about 1.5 million years ago. They used it to warm themselves, to cook food, and to frighten off wild animals.

Fire is a very fast chemical reaction called combustion. Combustion releases heat, light, and sound.

Ancient people used fire but they did not know what it was.

## Burning fuels

Fire is the easiest way to release energy from fuels. Fuels usually contain carbon and hydrogen. When you burn them, carbon dioxide and water are produced.

When any fuel burns, a chemical reaction happens between the fuel and oxygen.

In every flame, chemical reactions are taking place.

Bush fires can start if someone carelessly throws away a lit cigarette.

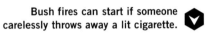

## Old ideas

In the ancient world, people believed that all things were made of four basic elements: fire, air, water, and earth. Later, scientists thought flammable (burnable) materials must contain a mysterious substance called 'phlogiston'.

Just over 200 years ago, the French chemist Antoine Lavoisier investigated combustion. He showed that combustion is a chemical reaction between a fuel and oxygen.

## Lack of oxygen

If there is not enough oxygen, a fire will not burn well. It will release carbon monoxide and lots of smoke. Carbon monoxide is a poisonous gas. Smoke pollutes the atmosphere.

135

# Wood and timber

Timber is the wood from felled (cut-down) trees. Timber is one of our most useful materials. It is used in house-building, for making furniture, building boats, and much more.

## Softwood

The most commonly used timber in building is called softwood. It is easy to work with because it is quite soft and easy to cut.

Softwood timber comes from evergreen trees such as firs, pines, cedars, and spruces. These trees grow in cool, northern regions of the world.

## Hardwood

Deciduous and tropical forests contain broad-leaved trees. Hardwood timber comes from broad-leaved trees such as oak, beech, chestnut, mahogany, ebony, and teak. These are valuable timbers.

The forest regions of the world.

**Key**

■ **coniferous forest** (evergreen conifers)

■ **deciduous forest** (trees lose leaves in autumn)

■ **tropical forest** (evergreen broad-leaved trees)

These trees are removed from the forest by truck.

## From forest to sawmill

Lumberjacks are people who cut down trees into logs. The logs are taken out of the forest by tractors, animals, cables, or water slides. Next they are taken to a sawmill by truck, railway wagon, or raft.

At the sawmill, the bark is removed. The logs are sawn into pieces of standard sizes. The timber is left to dry.

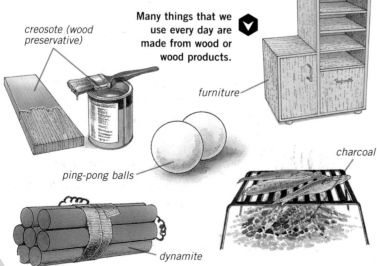

Many things that we use every day are made from wood or wood products.

creosote (wood preservative)

furniture

ping-pong balls

charcoal

dynamite

# Metals

It was around 5,000 years ago that humans discovered how to get metal out of rocks. They learnt to make metal tools. At first, people used copper and bronze. Then came iron, and finally steel.

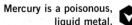
Mercury is a poisonous, liquid metal.

## Properties

Most metals are solids at room temperature. They all have a crystalline structure. This means that they are made of tiny particles arranged in a repeating, regular pattern. Pure metals are shiny when polished.

Mercury is the only metal that is liquid at room temperature.

Steel is very strong. It was used to build the London Eye in the UK.

## Strong metals

You can squeeze or stretch metals and they won't easily break. You can shape metals by hammering or rolling them. They can also be drawn out into thin wires. Metals can conduct electricity and heat.

| Name | Uses |
|------|------|
| Aluminium | Main material used in aircraft. Also used for window frames and soft-drink cans. |
| Copper | Used for electrical wires and water pipes, and sometimes on roofs. |
| Gold | Used in jewellery and electronics. |
| Iron | Most widely used metal. Can be made into steel. Used for a huge range of things, from bridges to paper clips. |
| Lead | Used for small, heavy weights and on roofs. In the past it was used in windows. |
| Silver | Used in jewellery, ornaments, and photographic film. |
| Uranium | Used as a fuel to produce nuclear energy. |

# Ceramics

Pottery is the most common type of ceramic. It has been around for many thousands of years. Bricks, tiles, and cement are also ceramic products.

Ceramics are usually made by baking sand and clay at high temperatures.

## Pottery

All pottery is made from clay. Different kinds of pottery are made from different kinds of clay. They are fired (baked) at different temperatures. Firing takes place in ovens called kilns.

## Ceramics in space

Space shuttles are covered in ceramic tiles. When space shuttles return to Earth, they must pass into Earth's atmosphere. This creates lots of heat. The tiles glow red-hot. The people inside stay safe because the tiles stop the heat from reaching them.

Ceramic tiles on space shuttles stop the shuttle from burning up completely as it enters Earth's atmosphere.

## Cement and concrete

Cement is a ceramic product. It is made by heating limestone and clay.

Concrete is a mixture of cement, sand, water, and gravel. When the concrete sets, it becomes very hard. Concrete is used to make roads and buildings.

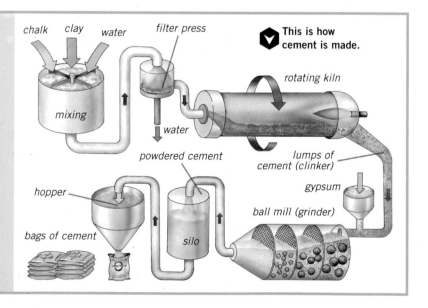

This is how cement is made.

chalk    clay    water    filter press

mixing

water

rotating kiln

powdered cement

lumps of cement (clinker)

gypsum

hopper

ball mill (grinder)

bags of cement    silo

# Glass

Glass has many uses, from windows and bottles to drinking glasses and laboratory equipment. Glass fibres are used to make plastic stronger and are even used in telephone cables.

The main ingredient in glass is silica. This is the same substance from which beach sand is made.

A glass blower makes a bubble in melted glass that can be turned into a vase or bowl.

## Making glass

Glass is made by heating sand, limestone rock, and soda ash. It becomes a red-hot liquid. When it cools it turns into transparent (see-through) glass.

## Glass properties

Glass is one of our most amazing materials. It is waterproof and it does not rot or rust. It is not damaged by most chemicals and it is easy to clean.

Glass is easily shaped into blocks, sheets, and fibres. Very fine glass fibres are used to carry telephone calls.

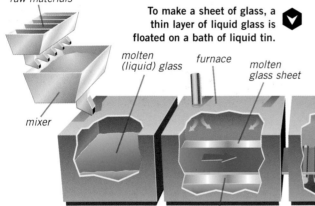

raw materials

To make a sheet of glass, a thin layer of liquid glass is floated on a bath of liquid tin.

molten (liquid) glass

furnace

molten glass sheet

mixer

cutter

finished sheet

rollers

heating stage

molten (liquid) tin

cooling area

## Special glass

Other ingredients can be added to the glass-making recipe. Adding lead oxide makes crystal glass. When crystal glass is cut properly, it gleams and sparkles like a diamond.

A chemical called boron can be added to the glass-making recipe. This makes glass that is not damaged by heat. It is used to make heat-resistant cookery bowls.

Coloured glasses are made by including metals in the glass-making recipe.

# Paper

As you read this book, you are looking at a material that started life in a forest. You are looking at paper. Paper is made from the wood of trees.

Paper is one of the greatest inventions of all time. It allows ideas and knowledge to be written down. They can be passed from one generation of people to the next.

## Making pulp

Cutting down trees into logs is the first stage in making paper. The bark is removed. Next, the logs must be turned into woodchips. Sometimes chemicals are added to the woodchips. This turns them into a kind of mush, called pulp.

▲ Paper usually comes from trees grown in Scandinavia or Canada.

## Types of paper

Different substances are added to pulp to make different types of paper:

- China clay makes paper heavier.
- Glue makes the paper easier to write on.
- Pigments give the paper colour.

◀ A worker in a paper-mill checks the wood pulp.

## Papermaking machine

Once all of the ingredients have been added, the pulp goes into the papermaking machine. The pulp is spread out on a wire mesh. Water can drain away and the pulp dries out.

Next, the damp paper is pressed and dried further. It is rolled to make the surface of the paper smooth.

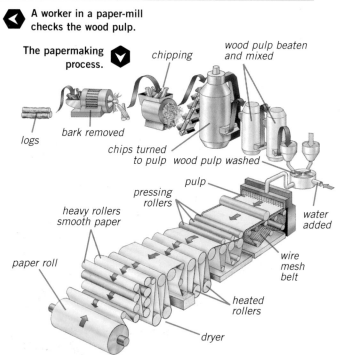

The papermaking process.

logs

bark removed

chips turned to pulp

chipping

wood pulp beaten and mixed

wood pulp washed

pulp

water added

pressing rollers

heavy rollers smooth paper

wire mesh belt

paper roll

heated rollers

dryer

# Plastics

We find plastics everywhere. We drink from plastic cups, fry food in plastic-coated pans, and carry shopping in plastic bags. Some clothes are even made from plastic.

Plastics are synthetic materials. Most plastics are made from crude oil.

## Making plastics

Plastics are made in factories. Small molecules are linked together into long chains. If a small molecule was the size of a daisy stalk, a plastic molecule would be up to 3,000 metres (9,850 feet) long.

warm plastic

air

mould

 Air is blown into warm plastic to make a bottle.

finished bottle

grains of plastic

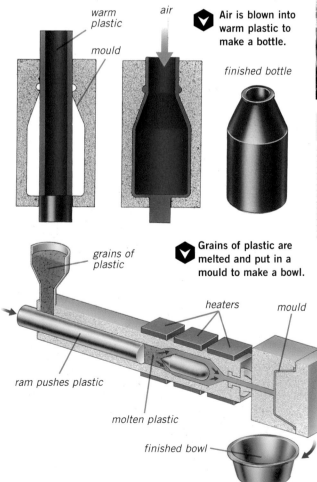 Grains of plastic are melted and put in a mould to make a bowl.

heaters

mould

ram pushes plastic

molten plastic

finished bowl

 Plastic bottles being made in a factory.

### FAST FACTS

**Types of plastic and their uses**
- [ ] PVC (window frames, shower curtains)
- [ ] Polythene (drinks bottles, plastic bags)
- [ ] Polystyrene (disposable cups, packaging foam)
- [ ] Nylon (clothes, carpets)

## Amazing plastics

Plastics have thousands of uses. Some plastics are not damaged by heat. They are made into kitchen worktops. Other plastics can be made into light, solid foams. Others are made into long strands. These can be woven into cloth.

# Fibres and textiles

Fibres can be natural or synthetic (man-made). Silk is a natural fibre that comes from silkworms. Synthetic fibres are mostly plastics (from oil). Nylon is a synthetic fibre.

When fibres are woven together, a fabric is produced. Silk fabric is just one example of the huge variety of textiles. We use textiles for clothes, carpets, parachutes, sails, and bandages.

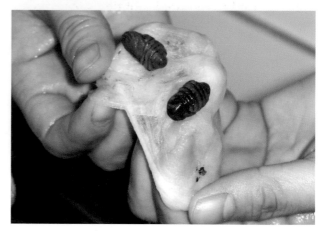

The silk has been unwrapped from the cocoons. One cocoon is made up of about 250 metres (820 feet) of fine silk thread.

## Silk

Silkworms eat huge quantities of mulberry leaves. After five weeks of eating, the worm starts to spin its cocoon. Two streams of liquid come from the worm. The liquid hardens into fine threads of one of the most prized fibres – silk.

## Rayon

Rayon is made either from cotton or from mashed-up wood. Parts of the cotton or wood are mixed with chemicals. Then the mixture is pumped through tiny holes. It solidifies into thin, strong fibres.

## Synthetics

Synthetic fibres, such as nylon and polyester, are made from plastic, which is a product of oil. They are often tougher than natural fibres, and they don't rot. They don't soak up water. This means that clothes made of synthetic fibres dry quickly.

## Natural fibres

Silk is one of two main fibres we get from animals. The wool from sheep is the other. Goats, camels, and llamas also produce useful fibres.

Cotton is by far the most important plant fibre. Cotton plants produce fibres in the seed pod. Linen is another plant fibre, made from the flax plant.

Nylon is made by melting plastic and then squeezing it through small holes. The nylon fibres become hard and are bundled together.

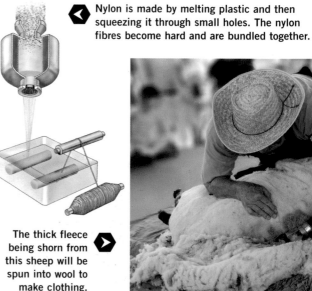

The thick fleece being shorn from this sheep will be spun into wool to make clothing.

## Textiles from fibres

The first step in making most textiles is to stretch and twist bundles of fibres together. This forms a yarn and is called spinning.

Weaving is the main method used to make fabric from yarn. In the weaving process, lengths of yarn are interlaced on a loom to form cloth. Other methods of making fabric from yarn include knitting and felting.

Both natural and synthetic fibres can be woven to make cloth. This loom weaves the fibres.

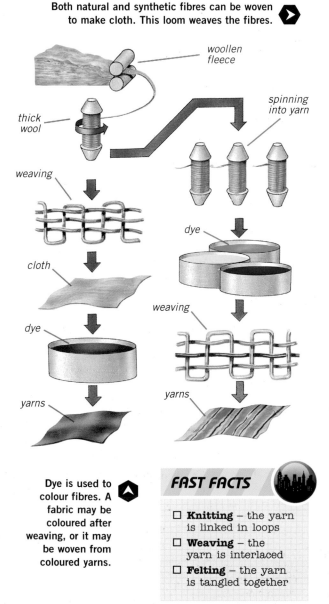

woollen fleece

thick wool

spinning into yarn

weaving

cloth

dye

dye

weaving

yarns

yarns

Dye is used to colour fibres. A fabric may be coloured after weaving, or it may be woven from coloured yarns.

### FAST FACTS

- ☐ **Knitting** – the yarn is linked in loops
- ☐ **Weaving** – the yarn is interlaced
- ☐ **Felting** – the yarn is tangled together

## Saris

The material for an Indian sari may come from a silkworm, or from a cotton plant. Or it may be a synthetic material made from oil. The cloth may be plain or printed. It may even have patterns made from gold or silver thread.

A sari is a long strip of unstitched cloth. Saris are the traditional clothing for Asian women.

## Textile properties

In general, textiles made from natural fibres are softer. Clothes made from natural fibres keep you warmer than those made from synthetic fibres.

Synthetic textiles are stronger, harder-wearing and do not crease as easily. Many modern textiles are made from a mixture of natural and synthetic materials.

# Rubber

Rubber is a stretchy material. Natural rubber is made from the sap of rubber trees. The main ingredient of man-made rubber is crude oil.

Rubber is used in tyres, some types of glove, and in shoes.

## Properties

Rubber is made of long molecules. The molecules are folded a bit like a spring. This is why rubber is stretchy.

Rubber is waterproof and it does not absorb (soak up) water. This is why it is good for its two main uses – car tyres and the soles of shoes.

A long, rubber bungee rope is tied to this girl's feet. Bungee ropes stretch and then spring back. ⬢

## Rubber trees

Rubber trees are grown in large groups called plantations. The trees ooze a milky sap called latex. People collect the latex by cutting the bark of the tree. The latex is mixed with other chemicals. It is rolled and squashed until it becomes solid rubber.

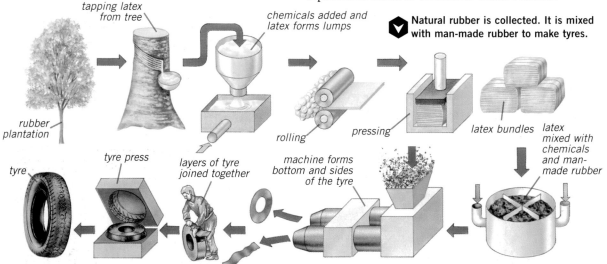

Natural rubber is collected. It is mixed with man-made rubber to make tyres. ⬢

tapping latex from tree

chemicals added and latex forms lumps

rubber plantation

rolling

pressing

latex bundles

latex mixed with chemicals and man-made rubber

tyre

tyre press

layers of tyre joined together

machine forms bottom and sides of the tyre

## Synthetic rubber

Crude oil forms under ground over millions of years. In factories, chemicals from the crude oil are mixed together. A chemical reaction produces a material that is very similar to natural latex.

⬢ A tyre press heats and hardens the rubber. This tyre press is releasing a new tyre.

# Construction

Construction is the building of roads, railways, bridges, dams, and tunnels. Humans have been constructing houses, temples, churches, and mosques for thousands of years.

These surveyors are measuring the height and shape of the land.

## Finding a site

Before construction can begin, a good site must be found. Surveyors measure the land accurately. They measure the height, size, and shape of the land. They check that the land is a good place to build a structure.

## Civil engineers

A civil engineer designs the road, dam, building, or bridge. They create detailed drawings of the whole structure.

## Shifting the muck

Bulldozers, excavators, and scrapers clear the site. They get rid of trees and big rocks, and flatten the land.

This giant excavator removes soil from the construction site.

## Firm foundations

Buildings need a strong, supporting base. This is the foundation. Foundations stop the structure from sinking into the ground.

- Raft foundations – This is a huge slab of concrete. It spreads the weight of a structure over a large area.

- Pile foundations –These are long columns sunk deep into the ground.

The structure is built on top of the foundations.

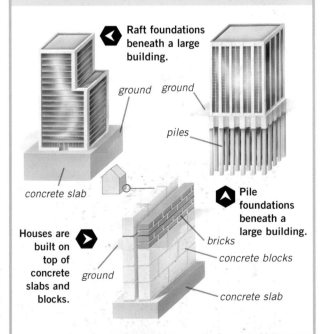

Raft foundations beneath a large building.

ground    ground

piles

concrete slab

Houses are built on top of concrete slabs and blocks.

ground

Pile foundations beneath a large building.

bricks

concrete blocks

concrete slab

# Roads and bridges

Every year, more than 50 million new vehicles roll on to the world's roads. Road systems are constantly being improved. Old roads are widened and new ones are built.

Bridges allow roads and railways to cross gorges, rivers, or even parts of the sea.

## Under construction

Before a road is built, a suitable route must be found. This must be agreed with local government, local people, and environmental groups.

Next, the route is cleared and levelled. Bridges, tunnels, and junctions are built.

## Road surfaces

Most road surfaces are a mixture of crushed stone and tar. This covering is called tarmac or asphalt.

Roads have a rounded top surface. This allows rainwater to run off. Drains along the edge carry the water away.

**DID YOU KNOW?**

There is a road that starts in Alaska and runs down through North America, into Central America, and on into South America. This road is 24,140 kilometres (15,000 miles) long!

Road-building uses many machines to prepare the ground and put down the surface.

Motorways are built so that other roads pass over or under them.

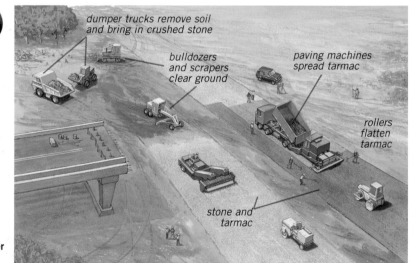

dumper trucks remove soil and bring in crushed stone

bulldozers and scrapers clear ground

paving machines spread tarmac

rollers flatten tarmac

stone and tarmac

## Motorways

Motorways have no traffic lights, roundabouts, or junctions. Motorways are built as level and as straight as possible. In this way, lots of traffic can travel quickly.

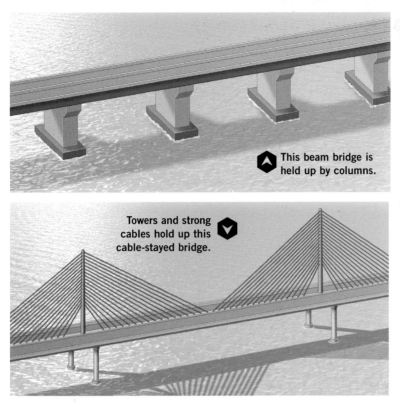

This beam bridge is held up by columns.

Towers and strong cables hold up this cable-stayed bridge.

## Beam bridges

The simplest and oldest type of bridge is the beam bridge. It is made out of a beam supported at each end.

Beams often sag in the middle. Simple beam bridges cannot cross a very wide gap. To cross a wide gap, a beam bridge needs columns to hold it up.

## Cable-stayed bridge

To cross a very wide gap, a beam bridge has tall towers. Cables attach the beam to the tall towers. This strengthens the bridge.

## Suspension bridges

In a suspension bridge, the road hangs from steel cables. The cables pass over tall towers. They are attached firmly at each end.

## Earthquakes and strong winds

Designers must make sure their bridges will not sway too much in the wind, or fall down if an earthquake happens. They make small models of the bridges and test them in wind tunnels. They give bridges added strength to protect them from earthquakes.

The road hangs on cables in this suspension bridge. Suspension bridges can cross the longest gaps.

Concrete arch bridges are strong.

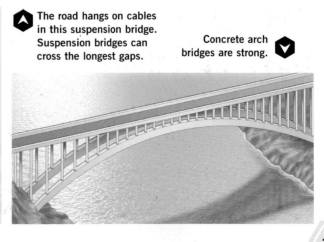

# Buildings

Buildings are created in a huge range of shapes and sizes. Traditional buildings are made of stone, clay, mud bricks, wood, and straw. Modern buildings are made of concrete, steel, bricks, and glass.

## Houses

Bricks have been used to build houses and walls for thousands of years. Traditional bricks are made of mud and dried in the Sun. Modern bricks are made of a clay mixture.

Many houses are built with wooden frames. These buildings can be made in sections. The sections are then put together on site.

**In this house, the outer walls were built first. They support the floors and the roof.** ▶

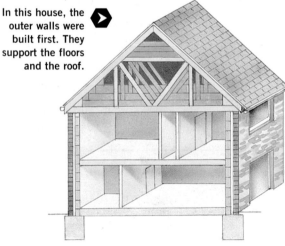

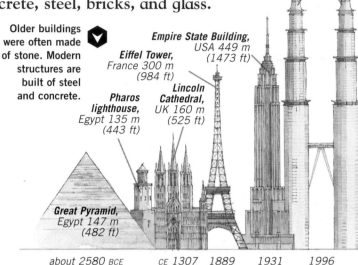

**Older buildings were often made of stone. Modern structures are built of steel and concrete.** ▼

*Petronas Towers, Malaysia 452 m (1,483 ft)*

*Empire State Building, USA 449 m (1473 ft)*

*Eiffel Tower, France 300 m (984 ft)*

*Lincoln Cathedral, UK 160 m (525 ft)*

*Pharos lighthouse, Egypt 135 m (443 ft)*

*Great Pyramid, Egypt 147 m (482 ft)*

about 2580 BCE    CE 1307    1889    1931    1996

## Domes

Some modern buildings have tent-like roofs. The material is pulled tight by steel cables. Domes are a good way to cover large areas. Sports stadiums are often covered by domes.

History Rising    Downtown at Burj Dubai

زڦی کیلومتر مربع علی وجـه الأرض
The most prestigious square kilometre on the planet

## Skyscrapers

Very tall buildings are called skyscrapers. Skyscrapers have a skeleton of steel girders (beams) around a concrete core. Steel is extremely strong. Skyscrapers' walls are often made of glass.

**The Burj Dubai will be the tallest building in the world when it is finished in late 2008. It will be more than 800 metres (2,625 feet) tall.** ▶

# Dams

Dams are the biggest of all man-made structures. Dams are built across rivers to stop flooding, to store water, or help create electricity.

## Making electricity

The water stored behind a dam is called a reservoir. This water is often used as a source of power. The water is released through turbines. The turbines spin generators that produce electricity. This is hydroelectric power.

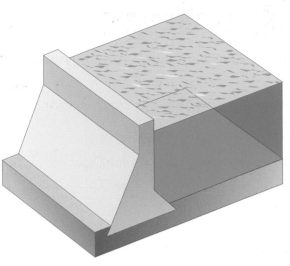

The triangle shape in a concrete dam is very strong. It must be strong enough to hold the water back.

The Hoover Dam is on the Colorado River, in the United States.

## Affecting the environment

Dams provide electricity and drinking water. They also protect people from deadly floods. But they can also bring problems.

When reservoirs are created, they flood towns and villages. People have to find new homes. Dams also reduce the flow of water down a river. This can affect wildlife and the surrounding environment.

## Three Gorges Dam

The Three Gorges Dam is one of the biggest dams in the world. The dam was built to stop flooding and to create electricity. It is built across the Yangtze River in China and is about 2.3 kilometres (1.4 miles) long and 185 metres (600 feet) high. It is made of 30 million cubic metres (10,590 million cubic feet) of concrete.

The reservoir behind the Three Gorges Dam is 300 km (375 miles) long.

# History of technology

Technology is the way in which we change the world to suit us. Scientists discover things about our world. Technologists find ways to put these discoveries to use.

## Wheels and ploughs

One of the earliest inventions was the wheel. It was invented in about 3500 BCE. The first wagon wheels were wooden discs cut from tree trunks. At around the same time, the plough was invented. Farmers in the Middle East first used ploughs to prepare soil for planting.

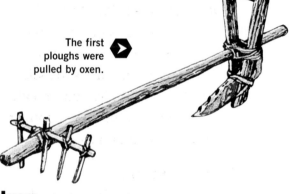

The first ploughs were pulled by oxen.

## Clothes

Much later, in 1767, the spinning jenny was invented. This machine could spin thread to make yarn. Yarn was woven into clothes. In 1935, the first man-made fibre was invented. It was called nylon, which is used to make tights.

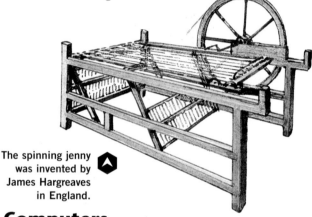

The spinning jenny was invented by James Hargreaves in England.

## Iron

In 1500 BCE, humans extracted (took) iron from rocks for the first time. They did this by heating rocks that contained iron in a furnace. This process is called smelting. People still use smelting today.

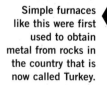

Simple furnaces like this were first used to obtain metal from rocks in the country that is now called Turkey.

furnace

## Computers

One of the earliest computers was built in 1944. The microchip was developed in 1971. Microchips are the 'brains' of computers. Since then, microchips have become smaller and far more powerful.

Nanotechnology is a very new technology. It is a way of working with individual atoms. This pattern is as small as a speck of dust. It was made using nanotechnology.

# Tools

Tools helps us to farm the land, build houses, and make thousands of everyday items.

Early humans used tools made of stone, wood, and bone. Today, most of the tools we use are made of metal or plastic.

## The first tools

Early humans first began using tools more than two million years ago. At first they used pieces of stone to chop and hammer things. In time, they began shaping stones into tools.

This is an early flint hand-axe.

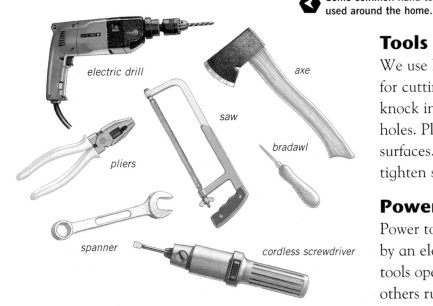

Some common hand tools used around the home.

electric drill

axe

saw

pliers

bradawl

spanner

cordless screwdriver

## Tools in the home

We use knives, scissors, and saws for cutting. We use hammers to knock in nails, and drills to make holes. Planes and files can smooth surfaces. Screwdrivers and spanners tighten screws and nuts.

## Power tools

Power tools are tools that are driven by an electric motor. Some power tools operate from mains electricity; others run on batteries.

## Tools in industry

In industry, huge power tools are used to cut and shape metal and rock. They are called machine tools. The work they carry out is called machining.

This huge machine tool cuts tunnels through rock.

# Microscopes

Microscopes magnify objects. They let us see tiny things that would otherwise be invisible to us.

Imagine being the first person to look at bacteria and tiny insects through a microscope. You would have seen creatures that looked like they were out of a scary horror movie!

## Lenses

Lenses are curved glass discs. They collect and bend light rays and make small objects look larger. Simple microscopes have two lenses. They are fixed at either end of a metal tube.

## Compound microscopes

Compound microscopes have many lenses. You look through the eyepiece lenses. Each objective lens (see below) has a different magnification. You can change the settings to use any of the objective lenses.

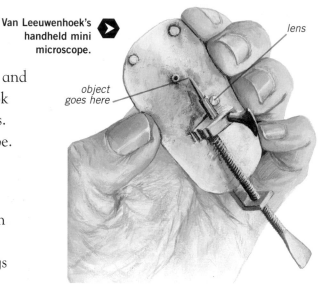

Van Leeuwenhoek's handheld mini microscope.

lens

object goes here

## Light

Compound microscopes have a lamp that shines light up through the object you are looking at. The object must be see-through, otherwise you can't see it using the microscope.

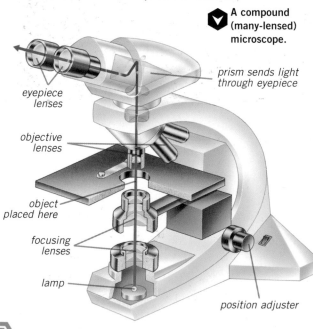

A compound (many-lensed) microscope.

prism sends light through eyepiece

eyepiece lenses

objective lenses

object placed here

focusing lenses

lamp

position adjuster

 Electron microscopes are very powerful microscopes. The object, such as this flea, does not need to be see-through.

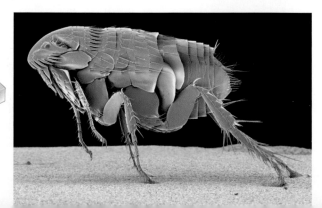

# Telescopes

Telescopes make things that are far away seem nearer. Astronomers use telescopes to study the stars. Birdwatchers use binoculars to spot birds. Binoculars are like a double telescope.

## How telescopes work

Most modern telescopes have two lenses. The objective lens collects light from distant objects. It produces an image inside the telescope. You look through the eyepiece lens. This lens makes the image inside the telescope look bigger.

This is how light passes through a telescope with lenses.

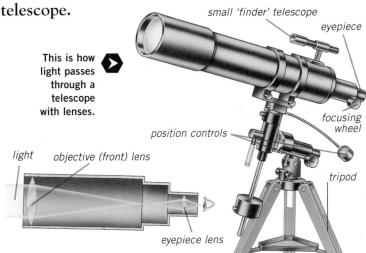

small 'finder' telescope

eyepiece

focusing wheel

position controls

tripod

light    objective (front) lens

eyepiece lens

## Faint objects

It is important to astronomers to be able to see things that are very faint, such as distant stars. Astronomical telescopes have very big lenses. The bigger the lens, the more light it can collect, and the more the astronomer can see.

**DID YOU KNOW?**

*The Keck I Telescope in Hawaii has a huge mirror that is 10 metres across.*

The Hubble Space Telescope shows more detail in the night sky (right hand image) than Earth-based telescopes (left hand image).

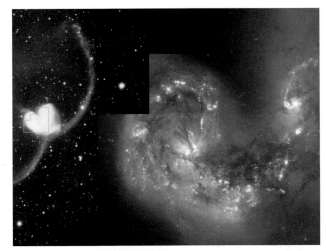

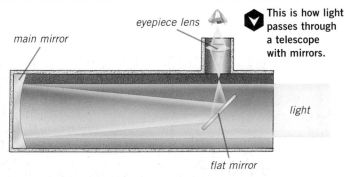

main mirror

eyepiece lens

This is how light passes through a telescope with mirrors.

light

flat mirror

## Mirrors

Large glass lenses are very heavy. So lenses can only be a certain size. A curved mirror can be used to gather the light instead. Telescopes with mirrors are called reflecting telescopes.

# Cameras and photography

Cameras are devices that take photographs. Photographs can be holiday snaps or pictures in books, newspapers, magazines, and exhibitions.

Photographs can show us a world that we do not normally see. High-speed cameras freeze fast-moving objects so that we can see what is happening.

## Taking a photograph

When you take a photograph, a shutter in the camera opens. It lets light into the camera. A lens collects and focuses the light to make the image.

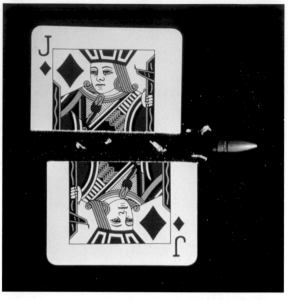

The shutter of a high-speed camera opens and closes very quickly to 'freeze' the movement of this bullet.

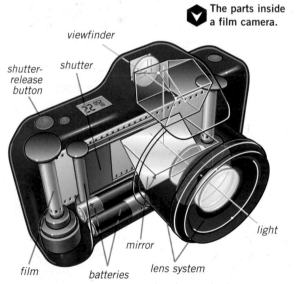

The parts inside a film camera.

viewfinder

shutter-release button

shutter

film

batteries

mirror

lens system

light

## Types of camera

There are two main types of camera – film cameras and digital cameras. Film cameras record the image on to photographic film. The film is sensitive to light. Digital cameras store the image on a memory card.

## Exposure

To take a good picture, a camera's shutter must let in just the right amount of light. It opens to a certain size and it opens for a certain amount of time. This is called the exposure.

At night or on cloudy days, the shutter must open wide and stay open longer to let in more light. On bright days, the shutter does not need to open as much.

Too little light makes the photo very dark (left). Too much light makes the photograph too bright (right).

## Stay sharp

To take a photograph that is sharp, the camera must focus properly. To focus, the lens changes position. Many cameras focus automatically. A tiny computer in the camera looks at how fuzzy the picture is. The computer tells the lens to move back and forth until the picture is sharp.

▼ A digital camera has a screen that shows the picture it will take.

Professional photographers use very advanced camera equipment. ▼

## Prints

Digital cameras store an image as a list of 1s and 0s on a memory card. This can be read by a computer, which displays the image. The image can be printed on to paper.

An image on a film is called a negative. Areas that were light in real life look dark on the film. Areas that were dark in real life look light on the film. A negative can be developed into a printed photograph.

film

▼ The negative image is changed into a photograph.

photograph

negative image of tree

◄ This memory card has been taken out of the digital camera.

positive image of tree

# Movies

A good movie takes you into a new world of action and adventure.

A movie is lots of still images shone on to a screen very quickly, one after another. You see it as a smoothly changing picture because the images trick your eyes.

## Filming a movie

Movie cameras capture the light coming from moving objects. Movie cameras freeze an image and store it. They do this over and over again. Most movie cameras store the images on film. Digital movie cameras store the images on a computer microchip.

## Projecting the movie

The projector at a cinema shines light through the film and on to a screen. Twenty-four images are projected on to the screen each second.

Digital movie projectors shine the movie at a screen that contains lots of tiny mirrors or crystals. At the moment, most movies are not shown in this way.

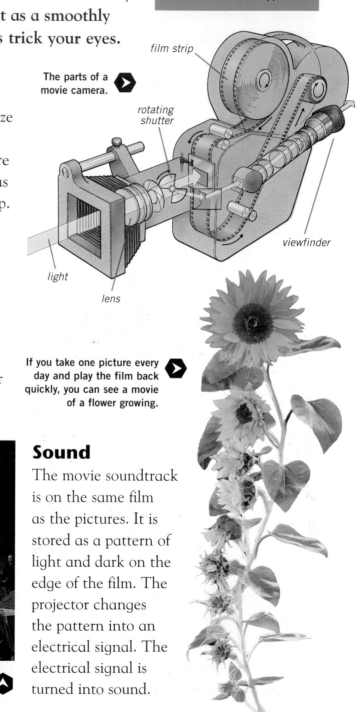

The parts of a movie camera. ▶

film strip

rotating shutter

viewfinder

light

lens

If you take one picture every day and play the film back quickly, you can see a movie of a flower growing. ▶

Filming a movie involves many people such as actors, camerapeople, sound workers, and directors. ▲

## Sound

The movie soundtrack is on the same film as the pictures. It is stored as a pattern of light and dark on the edge of the film. The projector changes the pattern into an electrical signal. The electrical signal is turned into sound.

# Communications

Speaking, writing, and signalling with your hands are all types of communication.

Today, information can travel round the world almost instantly. Machines such as telephones, televisions, computers, and radios help us communicate quickly over long distances.

## Telephones

Telephones let you speak to people who are far away. Telephones change the sound of your voice into signals. Usually, the signals are flashes of light. They are sent down optical fibres. Optical fibres are bundles of thin glass strands.

Optical fibres carry flashes of light.

## Satellites

Satellites are machines that circle the Earth. Communication satellites can be used to send signals around the world.

The satellite receives a signal such as a television sports broadcast.

**BIOGRAPHY**

**Samuel Morse**
Morse code was an early type of communication. It was invented in 1844 by the American inventor Samuel Morse (1791–1872). It is a system of dots and dashes. Different arrangements of dots and dashes are used to mean different letters and numbers.

| a ●▬ | b ▬●●● | c ▬●▬● | d ▬●● |
|---|---|---|---|
| e ● | f ●●▬● | g ▬▬● | h ●●●● |
| i ●● | j ●▬▬▬ | k ▬●▬ | l ●▬●● |
| m ▬▬ | n ▬● | o ▬▬▬ | p ●▬▬● |
| q ▬▬●▬ | r ●▬● | s ●●● | t ▬ |
| u ●●▬ | v ●●●▬ | w ●▬▬ | x ▬●●▬ |
| y ▬●▬▬ | z ▬▬●● | 1 ●▬▬▬▬ | 2 ●●▬▬▬ |
| 3 ●●●▬▬ | 4 ●●●●▬ | 5 ●●●●● | 6 ▬●●●● |
| 7 ▬▬●●● | 8 ▬▬▬●● | 9 ▬▬▬▬● | 10 ▬▬▬▬▬ |

The alphabet and numbers 1 to 10 in Morse code.

The Internet lets you communicate with people on the other side of the world.

It sends the signal on to another part of the Earth. A satellite dish on the side of your house collects the signal so that you can watch the broadcast on television.

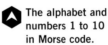

# Radio

Radio stations in every country broadcast programmes to billions of people. They send out their programmes as radio waves.

Radio waves are signals that are sent through the air from one place to another.

## Radio studio

In a radio studio, sound is turned into an electrical signal. This is called a sound signal. The sound signal is sent to a transmitter.

## Transmitters to your radio

A transmitter is a tall mast. The transmitter sends out the signal as radio waves. The radio waves travel through the air. The aerial on your radio picks up the radio waves. Loudspeakers play the sound.

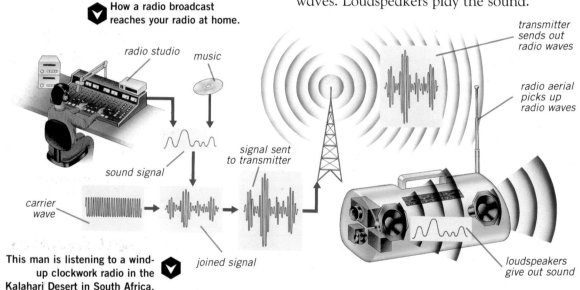

How a radio broadcast reaches your radio at home.

radio studio

music

sound signal

carrier wave

signal sent to transmitter

joined signal

transmitter sends out radio waves

radio aerial picks up radio waves

loudspeakers give out sound

This man is listening to a wind-up clockwork radio in the Kalahari Desert in South Africa.

## Digital radio

New transmitters can send out radio programmes as digital signals. To pick up the signal, you need a digital radio. The sound from a digital radio is clearer than from a traditional radio. Also, the radio automatically tunes in to all of the available radio stations. It displays which station you are tuned in to and may even tell you which programme you are listening to.

# Telephones

Telephones were first invented more than 100 years ago. They have changed a lot since then, but they still do the same job. They let you speak to people across long distances.

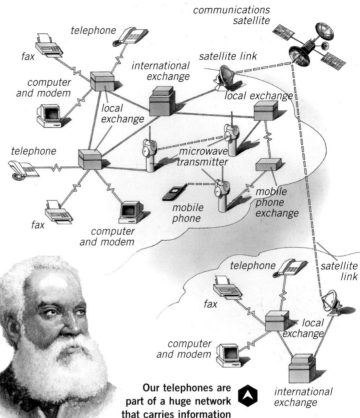

## Telephone exchanges

When you dial a phone number, the telephone sends the number to a place called an 'exchange'. Computers at your local exchange connect you to the person you are calling.

## How telephones work

When you speak into your handset, the sound of your voice is changed into a signal. This signal is sent through the telephone system to the other phone. At the other handset, the signal is changed back into sound.

Alexander Graham Bell invented the telephone in 1876.

Our telephones are part of a huge network that carries information all over the world.

## Mobile phones

Mobile phones use microwaves to send information from place to place. Mobile phones can make calls, send emails, store phone numbers, take photographs, and connect to the Internet.

Modern phones can play videos and music.

## Light fantastic

In modern phone networks, signals are sent down optical fibres. The signals are sent as flashes of light. In the past, electrical signals were sent down wires. Optical fibres can carry more calls than wires.

# Television

When we watch television, we can cheer our favourite sports teams or find out what is happening on the other side of the world. We can watch movies, soaps, and music television, too.

Almost every home in the developed world has a television set. In the developing world, the number of homes with television sets is rising fast.

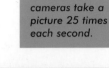

## On camera

A television camera works in a similar way to an ordinary camera. It captures light from a moving scene. The camera changes the pattern of light into electrical signals. Sound is added to the signals later.

A television programme being filmed. ▼

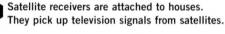

Satellite receivers are attached to houses. They pick up television signals from satellites.

## On screen

Most television sets break down the television signals into separate signals for red, blue, green, and sound. The colour signals blend together to create pictures on the screen. At the same time, the sound is reproduced through the speakers.

▼ This LCD (liquid crystal display) television screen uses up less electricity than a traditional television screen.

## To your home

Television signals are sent to your home as radio waves, by satellite, or through underground cables. Programmes are sent out by many different television stations. Your television has a tuner to pick out the signal from the station you want.

# Navigation

In the past, people found their way around by looking up at the sky. By day they looked at the Sun and by night they looked at the stars.

Today, other objects in the sky help us navigate. They are navigation satellites. Planes, ships, cars, and hikers use satellite navigation.

## Simple systems

Maps and compasses help people to find their way around. In the past, navigators also had devices called sextants. They measured the positions of the Sun and stars.

## GPS navigation

GPS stands for 'Global Positioning System'. The system uses 24 navigation satellites. They orbit the Earth and send out special radio signals.

A GPS receiver anywhere on Earth picks up signals from at least five of these satellites. The receiver uses the signals to work out its position.

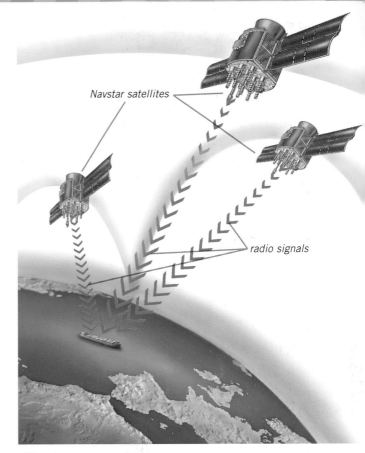

Navstar satellites

radio signals

▲ The receiver compares the satellites' signals to work out its position.

This in-car navigation system uses GPS to guide you from one place to another. ▼

## Use the stars

To use the stars to navigate, there are certain stars to look out for. If you live north of the Equator, look for the Plough. Two of its stars always point to the Pole Star, which points the way north.

The top star is the Pole star. It is in the north of the sky. ▶

pole star

plough constellation

# Compact discs

Compact discs (CDs) can store music, computer games, text (words), pictures, and computer software. You can play a CD in a stereo or in a computer.

## How information is stored

Each disc stores information as bumps on its surface. The bumps follow a spiral track. They start near the middle of the disc and end at the edge. The whole spiral track is over 8 kilometres (5 miles) long!

This is a bump on the surface of a CD. ▼

## Reading a CD

When you play a CD, a laser beam shines on to it. A laser is a type of light. The laser beam sweeps over the bumps. It reads the bumps and changes the pattern into electrical signals. The CD player turns the signals into sound.

CDs are useful because they store lots of information in a small space. ▼

## DVDs and recordable CDs

Digital videodiscs (DVDs) hold even more information than CDs. They do this by storing the information as smaller bumps.

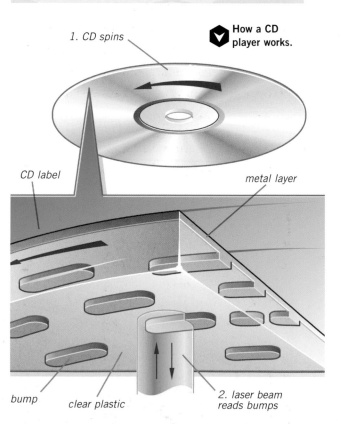

How a CD player works. ▼

1. CD spins

CD label

metal layer

bump     clear plastic     2. laser beam reads bumps

# Computers

Computers are machines that store and handle information. You can use them to play games, do your homework, and surf the Internet.

Computers can also control other machines such as dishwashers, space shuttles, and car production lines.

Computers control aircraft by sending electrical signals to the engine, wing flaps, and the tail flap (rudder). ▼

## Microchips

A computer takes in data (information). It processes the data using one or more microchips. A microchip is a thin slice of silicon that contains a complicated electronic circuit. Microchips are also called microprocessors.

▼ Tiny handheld computers, such as this one, can link to the Internet.

Designers use computers to make cartoon characters come to life. ▼

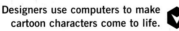

## Computers in industry

Computers are at the heart of most factories and businesses. Factories have computer-controlled machines and robots. Businesses use computers to keep track of orders, write letters, and keep accounts.

## Supercomputers

Supercomputers are extremely powerful computers. They are used for projects such as forecasting the weather. Many things happen at once in a weather system. Only a supercomputer can keep track of them.

# Hardware

A computer's hardware includes the main computer box, the screen, keyboard, mouse, and printer.

The main computer box contains all the electronic circuits that make the computer work. It also has sockets to plug in to other hardware devices.

Computer hardware.

Laptop computers have a rubber pad instead of a mouse.

## Screens

A computer's screen is also called a monitor. It helps us keep a check on how the computer is working. It displays information and pictures.

Modern computers have flat-screen monitors. They take up less space than older style monitors. Laptop screens contain liquid crystals that form words and images.

## Keyed up

Information is typed into a computer using a keyboard. Pressing a key on a keyboard makes two metal contacts touch each other. The computer then knows which key has been pressed.

**DID YOU KNOW?**

One day, scientists will be able to make plastic computers that can be rolled up and put in your pocket.

Bendy computers will have colour screens.

The laser in this mouse is red.

## Mouse

A mouse makes a computer easier to use. Instead of having to type everything, you can point and click anywhere on the screen.

Most mice have a laser light underneath them. Older mice have a ball inside that rolls as you move the mouse around. When you move a mouse, a cursor (arrow) moves on the screen.

# Software

Computer software means the programs that tell the computer what to do. A computer program can be thought of as a recipe. It is a list of instructions that makes the computer do the job you want it to.

## Programs

Computer programs can do really useful things. Word processing progams let us type letters. Database programs let us store information. Spreadsheet programs let us do calculations.

Computer programs can also control a space rocket, manage your washing machine cycle, or change traffic lights.

## Viruses

Not all software is useful. Computer viruses are programs that invade computer systems. Some viruses delete everything on your computer. Others delete all of your pictures or music files.

 Some computer programs describe how web pages on the Internet should look.

## Microsoft

In the early 1980s, a company called IBM designed a personal computer (PC). But their computer had no software. They asked a tiny company called Microsoft to write their software. This company was run by an American called Bill Gates. Microsoft grew and Bill Gates became the richest man in the world.

In a supermarket, databases track the products that are sold and the products that must be ordered in from suppliers.

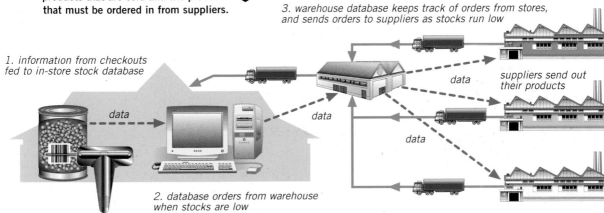

3. warehouse database keeps track of orders from stores, and sends orders to suppliers as stocks run low

1. information from checkouts fed to in-store stock database

suppliers send out their products

data

data

data

data

2. database orders from warehouse when stocks are low

# Internet

The Internet is a huge computer network. It connects you to people all around the world.

You can use the Internet to send emails, download music, or play computer games. And you can find out almost anything you might want to know.

## Connecting to the Internet

To use the Internet you need a computer and a link to the network. The link can be a broadband connection or a modem and telephone line. Libraries, schools, and Internet cafes may have computers that you can use.

## Web pages

The World Wide Web is part of the Internet. It is made of thousands of individual computers called web servers. They store information in files called websites.

Search engines help you find the websites you are interested in. If you are interested in dinosaurs, enter the word 'dinosaur' in a search engine. It will give you a list of sites on that subject.

## Email

Sending messages by email is very popular. You can write messages as long or as short as you like. You can 'attach' all sorts of other computer files – a picture, a movie, a sound file, or a computer program.

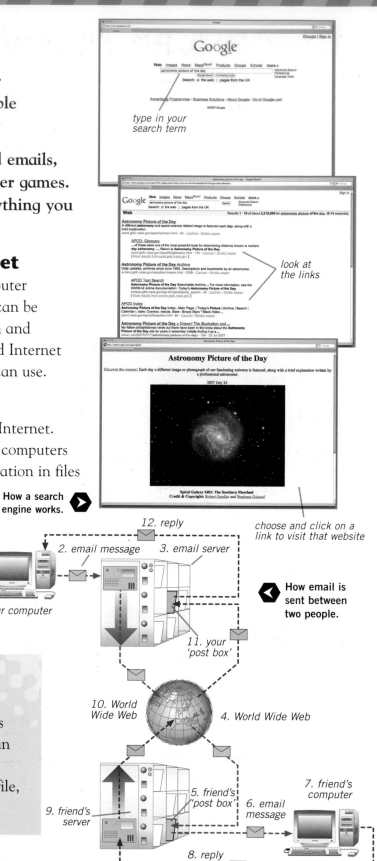

type in your search term

look at the links

**Astronomy Picture of the Day**

Discover the cosmos! Each day a different image or photograph of our fascinating universe is featured, along with a brief explanation written by a professional astronomer.

2007 July 24

Spiral Galaxy M83: The Southern Pinwheel
Credit & Copyright: Robert Gendler and Stephane Guisard

choose and click on a link to visit that website

**How a search engine works.** ❯

12. reply

2. email message

3. email server

**How email is sent between two people.** ❮

1. your computer

11. your 'post box'

10. World Wide Web

4. World Wide Web

9. friend's server

5. friend's 'post box'

6. email message

7. friend's computer

8. reply

# Computer graphics

Computer graphics are pictures created on computers. Movies such as *Shrek* and *Ratatouille* were made on computers.

Vehicles, buildings, bridges, and clothes can all be designed using computer graphics.

A computer makes 24 pictures for every second of the movie.

## Materials and money

Computer graphics let you try out lots of different designs until you have one that is just right. You don't have to make and test each one. This can save money and materials.

Imagine you want to design a new style of shoe. The computer can work out just how much material you need.

## How it works

The designer presses a special pen on a rectangular pad called a graphics tablet. The computer screen displays the drawing.

The drawing is saved in the computer's memory. It is then possible to look at the design from a different angle, or colour it differently.

This man is using computer graphics to design a car.

This computer design shows a future NASA space shuttle.

## Practice makes perfect

Computers let you check how well your design will work. For example, it could check how well a bridge design will stand up to high winds. This is called simulation.

167

# Robots and AI

A robot is an automatic machine. Robots do not make mistakes or get tired. They can also work just about anywhere.

If a robot can make decisions for itself, we say it has artificial intelligence (AI).

## Robot workers

Robots do jobs that are too repetitive for people to do. In factories, robots carry out tasks that have to be done over and over again, 24 hours a day.

Robots are also used for dangerous tasks. They are used for finding bombs and making them safe.

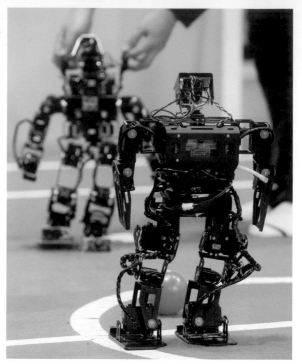

Artificial intelligence scientists test out their ideas by building robot football players.

**DID YOU KNOW?**

A new vacuum cleaner has been invented. It can wander around a room on its own, sucking up dust and dirt.

## Smart and smarter

A robot in a factory can be 'trained' by a human. It can copy the movements the human makes.

Scientists are now trying to make robots more clever, so that they can do more jobs. The main aim is to build robots that have AI and can work out for themselves how to do things.

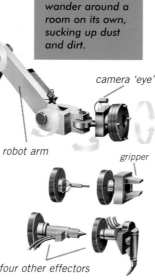

Most robots have an arm that can be fitted with several different effectors (hands).

joint

camera 'eye'

robot arm

gripper

joint

four other effectors

controller

This home robot can detect burglars, noises, smells, and temperature changes. It reports back to its owner by mobile phone.

**FAST FACTS**

**Parts of a robot**
- ☐ Controller – the robot's brain
- ☐ Sensors – the robot's sight, hearing, and sense of touch
- ☐ Effectors – the robot's hands

# Virtual reality

Virtual reality involves creating a space, such as a room or a cave, inside a computer's memory. To get inside the space, you must wear a helmet.

You can walk around the space, listen to sounds, and even touch the new world that the computer has created.

The parts of a virtual reality helmet.

adjustable strap

tiny video screen (one for each eye)

headphones

## Three dimensions

The helmet contains two tiny video screens. When you put the helmet on, one video screen is in front of each of your eyes. The images are slightly different in each screen. This makes you see a three-dimensional (3D) effect.

## Uses for virtual reality

Virtual reality lets designers get a feel for buildings or cars that have not even been built yet. Players of computer games can use virtual reality. It makes the game very realistic.

Engineers can 'walk around' their design ideas.

## Movement and sound

When you move your head, the images that you see move too. This makes you feel that you are in the new environment. Speakers in the helmet let you hear sound all around you.

## Touch

Virtual reality gloves let you touch the new environment. When you 'push' on something, tiny balloons in the glove inflate. They press on your hand and it feels like you have really pushed something!

The virtual reality glove has connections to the helmet and computer.

169

# Farming

Farming is growing crops and raising animals to provide food and other products.

Different types of farming are carried out in different parts of the world. Farmers grow crops or keep animals that are suited to the land and climate.

Combine harvesters cut cereal crops such as wheat and rape.

## Growing crops

Farmers crops include cereals, vegetables, fruit and nuts, sugar, oil, tea, and cotton.

Wheat, rice, and maize are the most important cereal crops. They provide the staple (basic) food for most people.

## Farm animals

Beef cattle are raised for their meat. Dairy cattle are raised for their milk. Sheep, pigs, and chickens are also important farm animals.

| CROPS | | | |
|---|---|---|---|
| rice | sugar | coffee | cotton |
| China India | India Cuba | Brazil Colombia | China USA |

| LIVESTOCK | | | |
|---|---|---|---|
| cattle | sheep | pigs | goats |
| India | Australia | China | China (meat) India (milk) |

This table shows the top producing countries for different products.

## Outdoors and indoors

Most farm animals are raised in fields or on ranches. A ranch is a farm where huge numbers of animals are kept in wide open spaces.

Some farm animals are kept indoors under controlled conditions. Pigs and chickens are often farmed in this way. Indoor farming produces meat and eggs cheaply. Many people think that it is cruel.

This farmer is using a water buffalo to plough his rice paddy field in Vietnam.

## Fertilizers

As crops grow, they take the goodness from the soil. Fertilizers are designed to put back the goodness so that future crops can also grow well.

Farmyard manure and sewage sludge are natural fertilizers. Artificial fertilizers are made from chemicals.

Manure is scattered over a field by a mechanical spreader.

A crop-sprayer flies low to spray pesticide over a crop.

## Moving around

Farmers in the tropics grow rice, millet, manioc, and maize. After about a year, the goodness in the soil has been used up. Instead of using fertilizers, the farmers move on, clear fresh land, and plant a new crop.

## Pesticides

Pesticides are chemicals that are sprayed on crops to get rid of damaging insects or weeds. However, these chemicals can also harm other wildlife.

The two-spot spider mites damage the leaves of the crops. The red spider mites kill the two-spot spider mites.

cucumbers

two-spot spider mite

leaf damage

red spider mite

corn

tomatoes

## Pest control

Two-spot spider mites are pests. They damage cucumber, tomato, and maize plants. One way to control these pests is to release red spider mites. The red spider mites catch and eat the two-spot spider mites.

# Mining

Mining is getting rocks and minerals out of the ground. People mine for diamonds, gold, coal, and metal ores. Metal ores are rocks that contain metals.

## Surface mining

Some ores are found near the surface of the ground. Mining at the surface is called opencast mining.

Huge excavators remove the soil and rock. If the ore or coal deposit is soft, it can be dug out. If it is hard, it is broken up by explosives.

 Mining is a dangerous and dirty job.

## Miners

Large underground mines have hundreds of kilometres of tunnels. There may be lifts and railways to carry miners. Shafts supply fresh, cool air for the miners to breathe. Other shafts have skips to lift out the rock.

Different methods of mining are needed to reach mineral or coal deposits.

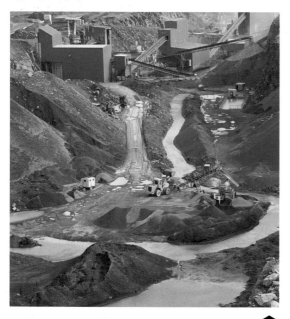

An opencast mine.

## Deep underground

Many rocks and minerals are found deep under the ground. To reach them, a shaft and tunnels are dug. Explosives are used to break up the rocks. The pieces are transported to the surface.

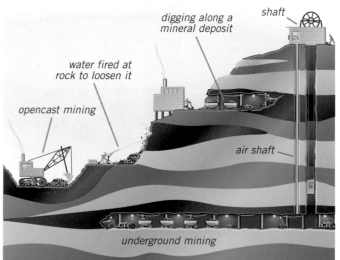

shaft

digging along a mineral deposit

water fired at rock to loosen it

opencast mining

air shaft

underground mining

# Coal

Coal is a hard, black substance. When it is heated, it catches fire and burns fiercely. It is found in deposits in the ground and is a very important fuel.

Coal is a dirty fuel. Burning coal is contributing to global warming.

## Coal formation

Coal is a fossil fuel. Fossil fuels form over millions of years from the remains of living things. Coal is formed from the remains of trees and plants. The dead plants piled up and other materials settled on top. The plants were squashed. Eventually, they hardened and turned into coal.

## Running out

Coal is found in thick layers called seams. The seams can be deep underground or near the surface. Coal is valuable and is mined all across the world. But it will not last forever. The Earth's coal supply will be used up in the next 200 years.

## Using coal

Many power stations burn coal to produce electricity. Coal is also burned in the steel and cement-making processes.

Coal is also a source of chemicals that can be used to make soap, dyes, medicines, pesticides, and other products.

This coal-fired power station is in the Hebel Province in China.

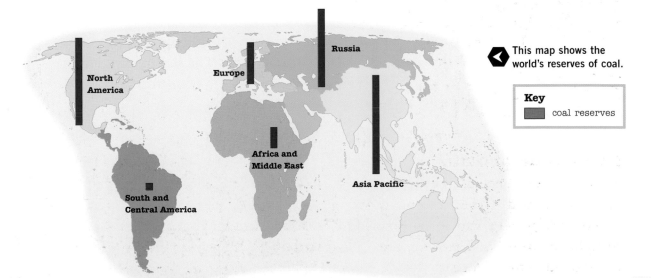

North America

Europe

Russia

Africa and Middle East

Asia Pacific

South and Central America

This map shows the world's reserves of coal.

**Key**
coal reserves

# Oil and gas

Crude oil is a black liquid found deep beneath the ground. It is a very valuable fuel that is used to power cars, buses, and other machines. It also contains many useful chemicals.

Natural gas is often found underground with crude oil. It is also an important fuel.

## Formation

Oil and gas are fossil fuels. They formed over millions of years from the buried remains of animals and plants that lived in ancient seas.

Today, oil and gas are found trapped in holes in the rock, deep under the land and under the seabed.

Russia

Europe

North America

Middle East

Asia Pacific

Africa

South and Central America

◀ A drill digs towards an oil and gas deposit. The deposit may be hundreds of metres down.

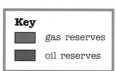

**Key**

gas reserves

oil reserves

▲ Most oil and gas is found in the Middle East.

engine

drill pipe

layers of rock

deposits of oil and gas

drill bit

## Drilling for oil

Experts study layers of rock beneath the surface of the Earth. If they think they have found some oil, they set up a drilling rig. The sharp drill can dig down up to 60 metres (195 feet) every hour.

## Hitting oil

If the drill meets oil or gas, the fuel flows back up the shaft. The shaft becomes an oil well or a gas well. On land, pipes are attached to the top of the well. The pipes take away the oil or gas. At sea, an oil rig must be set up.

## Oil rigs

An oil rig is a huge platform out at sea. Pipes go down from the platform to the oil well on the seabed.

If the sea is deep, the oil rig floats on the water. If the sea is shallow, the oil rig stands on long legs that reach right down to the seabed.

## Using oil

Once the oil has been taken out of the ground, it is transported to a refinery. Oil contains lots of useful substances such as diesel and petrol. A refinery is a place where the substances are separated out.

An oil rig.

Gas burns and releases heat. The heat cooks the food.

**DID YOU KNOW?**

Oil and gas will not last forever. Experts think that they will run out by the year 2050.

At an oil refinery the crude oil is separated into many different products. The main ones are fuels (such as liquid petroleum gas (LPG), petrol, paraffin, and diesel), lubricating oils, and bitumen for surfacing roads.

## Using gas

The gas is transported to a place called a gas terminal. From there it is pumped to homes and factories. In homes, gas is used for cooking and heating. Some power stations burn gas to produce electricity.

# Industry

Industry is the work that people do to produce goods or services. Farming, manufacturing (making things), and tourism are different types of industry.

All industries are either primary, secondary, or service industries.

## Primary industries

In a primary industry, natural materials are taken from the Earth. The natural materials include oil, rocks, wood, and crops. Mining, farming, and fishing are all primary industries.

## Secondary industries

In a secondary industry, the natural material is made into a new product. Manufacturing is a secondary industry. Manufacturing industries make products that people buy, such as cars.

## Service industries

Not all industries make products. Some offer a service instead. Selling goods made by manufacturing is a service industry. Banking, nursing, education, and tourism are also service industries.

▼ Primary industries produce natural materials. Secondary industries make the materials into products that consumers (people) use.

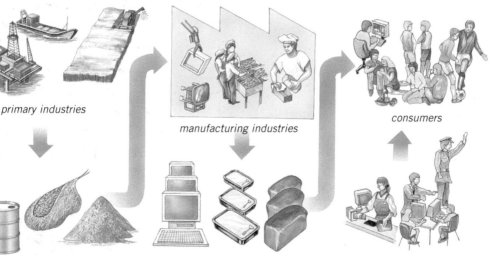

primary industries

manufacturing industries

consumers

raw materials

products

service industries

## Revolution in industry

In Europe, until about 250 years ago, most goods were made at home. They were sold locally. This kind of industry is called a cottage industry.

Over time, people invented machines that could do the work faster. In 1771, the first factory was built. Factories grew bigger and better (see left). This was called the Industrial Revolution.

# Metalworking

Metalworking is the shaping of metal into objects that we use.

When metal is heated, it becomes soft or runny. It can then be shaped into useful objects such as a car door, metal toy, ship hull (body), or a wheel.

## Forging

To forge a piece of metal, it is first heated until it is soft. Next it is hammered or squashed. When it cools, it keeps its new shape. Horseshoes and car doors are made in this way.

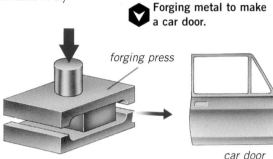

▼ Forging metal to make a car door.

*forging press*

*car door*

## Moulding

Metal is heated until it is a liquid. Then it is poured into a mould. When it cools and hardens, it takes the shape of the mould. Moulding is used to make train wheels and ships' propellers.

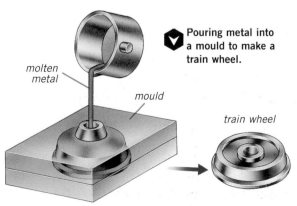

▼ Pouring metal into a mould to make a train wheel.

*molten metal*

*mould*

*train wheel*

▲ A red-hot sheet of metal is rolled.

## Rolling along

To make objects such as a ship's hull or a car's body, you need large, thin sheets of metal. The metal starts off as a thick slab. It is heated. In a rolling mill, the hot slab is passed backwards and forwards through heavy rollers.

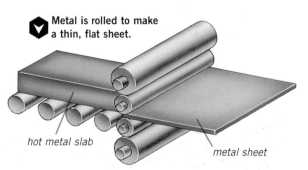

▼ Metal is rolled to make a thin, flat sheet.

*hot metal slab*

*metal sheet*

A slab that was 10 metres (33 feet) long could end up as a sheet 2 millimetres (0.08 inches) thick and 1.5 kilometres (0.9 mile) long.

# Printing

Printing is the process of reproducing words and pictures on paper. Books, magazines, and newspapers are produced by printing.

In the oldest printing method, raised letters were coated with ink. They were pressed against a sheet of paper. Today, a process called litho printing is used.

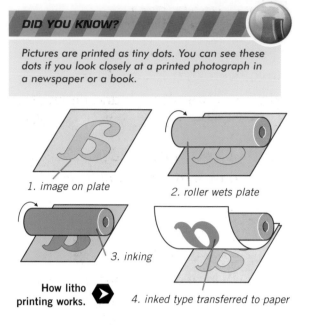

1. image on plate

2. roller wets plate

3. inking

4. inked type transferred to paper

How litho printing works.

## Printing colour

(a)

To print a colour picture, four versions of the picture are created. One is yellow, one is cyan (blue), one is magenta (pinky red), and one is black. This is called colour separation.

(b)

A printing plate is made for each of the versions. The yellow plate is printed first, followed by the cyan plate, then the magenta. The black plate prints last and produces the full-colour picture.

(c)

(d)

Yellow (a), cyan (b), magenta (c), and black (d) are used to create a full-colour picture.

## Litho printing

The image to be printed is put on a screen called a printing plate. The plate is wetted and inked by rollers. The ink only sticks to the image. A new roller transfers the ink image to the paper.

## Newspapers

Newspapers are designed on a computer. The pages are sent to the printer as electronic files. The printer uses the files to make printing plates.

After the text is written and photographs taken, the newspaper is designed on a computer. It is checked over and then printed.

designer

editors check the newspaper content

newspapers printed

# Science

The three main sciences are physics, chemistry, and biology. Biology is the science of life. Physics and chemistry study the physical, non-living world.

Earth science is the study of the Earth. Astronomy is the study of space.

## Physics

In physics, scientists study matter and energy. Everything that exists is made of matter. Anything that happens involves energy of some sort. Heat, electricity, light, and sound are types of energy.

 A chemist testing chemicals in a laboratory.

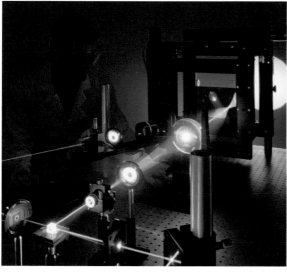

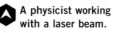 A physicist working with a laser beam.

## Chemistry

In chemistry, scientists study the chemicals that make up our world. They investigate the changes that take place when these substances react together.

Chemists find ways of making useful products such as new plastics, detergents, and medicines.

## Biology

In biology, scientists study living things. They investigate plants, animals, and the places in which they live. They also study how different living things affect each other. This is called ecology.

Biologists that study plants are called botanists.

## Earth and space sciences

The main Earth science is geology. Geologists study the Earth, what it is made from, and how it changes.

Astronomers study planets, stars, and galaxies.

# Transport

Transport includes cars, buses, trains, aeroplanes, and ships.

Two hundred years ago, most people did not travel far from their homes. This changed when engines were invented. Engines power most forms of transport. Today travel is easier, quicker, and cheaper than in the past.

## Cars

Cars are quick and convenient. But they also jam our roads and produce gases that pollute the air. In the future we may drive cars powered by the Sun or by electricity.

Cars have changed a lot in the last 100 years.

## Trains

Trains are better for the environment than cars. They can carry lots of people and they are fast. As traffic jams on the roads get worse, trains are becoming more popular.

*first ever car*

*people carrier*

▲ The French TGV train can travel at speeds of over 515 kph (320 mph).

### Key dates

- ☐ 1804 First successful steam train is built.
- ☐ 1807 First successful steamboat is built.
- ☐ 1885 First motor car is built.
- ☐ 1903 First aeroplane is flown.
- ☐ 1959 First hovercraft is designed.
- ☐ 1969 The Boeing 747 jumbo jet makes its first flight.
- ☐ 2005 The Super Jumbo makes its first flight.

## Planes

For really long journeys, most people travel by plane. At peak times, airports are filled to overflowing. A new 'Super Jumbo' can carry over 600 passengers.

## Ships

Ships are the best way to transport heavy loads over very long distances. The biggest ships are oil tankers. They can be 0.5 kilometres (0.3 miles) long.

The Super Jumbo A380 is a double-decker plane. It has seats on two levels. ▼

### BIOGRAPHY

**Christopher Columbus**
In 1492, Christopher Columbus sailed across the Atlantic Ocean. He discovered the 'New World' (America). His journey by ship took more than a month.

# Ships and submarines

Ships and boats have been transporting people and goods for thousands of years. People take holidays on cruise ships, and huge oil tankers transport oil all over the world.

Submarines travel beneath the waves. Some submarines explore the ocean floor. Others carry weapons.

A cruise ship can carry more than 3,000 people.

## Sails

Sailing boats are pushed along by the force of the wind. Sailing boats are mainly used for leisure or racing.

A sailing boat has a keel to give it stability.

keel

## Engines

Modern ships have engines. The engines turn propellers, which push the ship along. Cruise ships, cargo ships, and container ships are powered in this way.

Cargo ships carry goods such as grain and oil. Container ships carry large metal containers. The containers hold goods such as clothing or books. The goods will be sold in a foreign country.

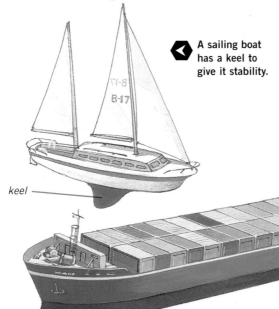

Container ships are the most common cargo ships.

## Under the waves

Submarines dive underwater. To dive down, tanks in the submarine fill up with water. To rise to the surface, air is pumped into the submarine's tanks. Some submarines can stay underwater for months at a time.

These new German submarines are in the Baltic Sea.

# Trains

Trains are the fastest type of land transport. They can carry lots of passengers or heavy goods.

Trains are made up of a locomotive and carriages. The locomotive pulls the carriages.

## Powering along

Early locomotives ran on steam power. They burned coal to heat water and turn it into steam. These trains produced lots of smoke and were very dirty.

Today's locomotives are powered by diesel fuel, electricity, or a mix of the two.

## The track

Trains have steel wheels that run along a steel track. The steel track sits on strong blocks called sleepers.

In most countries, the two rails of the track are 143.5 centimetres (56.5 inches) apart. The distance is called the gauge. Other gauges are used in some countries.

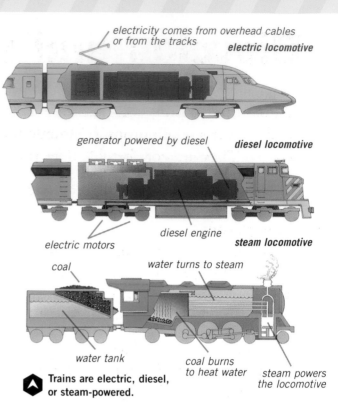

electricity comes from overhead cables or from the tracks

**electric locomotive**

generator powered by diesel

**diesel locomotive**

electric motors

diesel engine

**steam locomotive**

coal

water turns to steam

water tank

coal burns to heat water

steam powers the locomotive

Trains are electric, diesel, or steam-powered.

A maglev train uses magnets to float above the track.

A heavily loaded train pulls its cargo through the Rocky Mountains in the USA.

## Going underground

Underground trains travel beneath our streets. The London Underground in the UK is the world's largest underground railway. It has more than 400 kilometres (248 miles) of track.

# Bicycles and motorcycles

Bicycles are cheap to buy, fun to use, and they cause no pollution. Racing bikes are very light. They travel quickly over smooth ground. Mountain bikes are heavier. They are comfortable over rough ground.

A motorcycle is a bicycle with an engine.

**DID YOU KNOW?**

Mountain bikes can have up to 24 gears. Gears make it easier to cycle up very steep hills.

## Bike power

Bicycles are powered by your muscles. When you push down on the pedals, the chain turns. The chain drives the wheels.

Bicycle frames are made from metals such as steel. Expensive bicycles use a very lightweight metal called aluminium.

Parts of a mountain bike. ▶

new frame designs use very lightweight materials

suspension

lightweight wheels

## Mountain bikes

Mountain bikes have a very strong frame. They have chunky tyres to keep them steady on bumpy ground. They let you go where you want – along muddy tracks, down rocky slopes, and over potholes.

## Motorcycles

Motorcycles are a cross between a bicycle and a car. They are steered by the front wheel, like a bicycle. They have a petrol engine and powerful brakes, like a car. Motorcycles are used for fun as well as for transport.

This jumping motorbike is competing in a race. ▶

# Cars and trucks

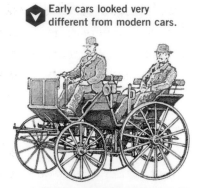

Early cars looked very different from modern cars.

There are more than 500 million cars in the world. There are also millions of trucks and buses.

Cars play an important part in people's lives. We drive our cars to work, to the shops, and to our leisure activites. Trucks transport goods long distances.

## Engine power

Most cars have either a petrol or diesel fuel engine. Trucks have diesel fuel engines. When vehicles burn fuel, they produce carbon dioxide gas. The gas builds up in the air and acts like a blanket around the Earth. It traps extra heat and causes global warming.

## Future fuels

In the future, cars could be powered by the Sun or by a type of battery called a fuel cell. Fuel cells make electricity. They do not release gases that damage the environment.

Racing cars have 'wings' at the front and back. These help the cars stick to the road at high speeds.

**Key**

- ▮ engine runs on petrol or diesel
- ▮ transmission takes power to wheels
- ▮ gearbox allows car to drive at different speeds
- ▮ cooling system
- ▮ exhaust
- ▮ steering
- ▮ brakes
- ▮ electrical system
- ▮ suspension joins wheels to the body

## Parts of a car

A car is powered by its engine. The transmission takes the power from the engine to the wheels. Gears help a car drive well at different speeds.

When you push the accelerator pedal, the car speeds up. When you press the brakes, the car slows down. Turning the steering wheel changes the car's direction.

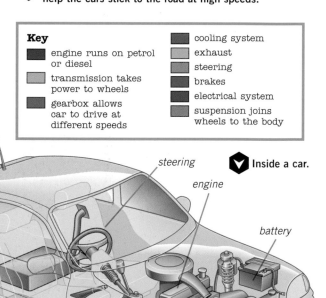

Inside a car.

steering

engine

battery

exhaust

gearbox

suspension (to create a smooth ride)

brakes

cooling system

## Accidents and safety

Cars can be very dangerous. Every year, car accidents kill more than one million people. Seat belts, safety glass, and air bags make cars safer for passengers.

## Crash tests

Before a new type of car is sold, the manufacturer carries out a crash test. They put a dummy in the car and drive the car into a wall. The front part of the car is crushed. This part is called the crumple zone.

**You can see the crumple zone at the front of the car.** ▶

The crumple zone helps to keep the driver safe. It takes most of the force of the crash and protects the passengers. The crash test checks that the crumple zone works properly.

## Trucks

Large trucks are made up of a cab and a body. The cab is where the driver sits. The body attaches to the back of the cab. The truck hinges (bends) at the point where the two pieces join. This makes it easier for the truck to get round corners.

When a mechanic needs to work on a truck's engine, the cab must be tipped forwards.

**This is how the cab tips forwards.** ▶

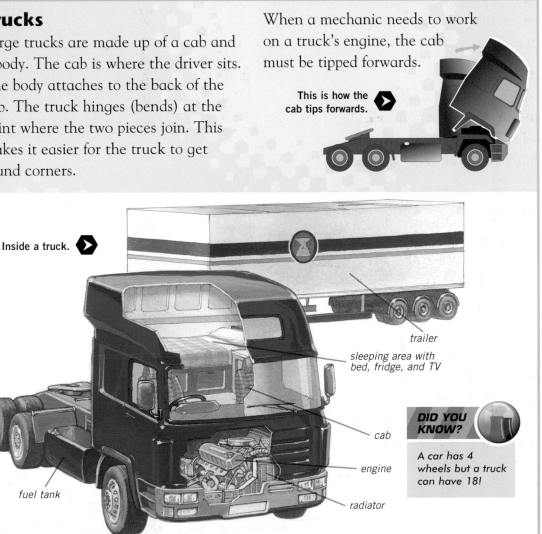

**Inside a truck.** ▶

trailer

sleeping area with bed, fridge, and TV

cab

engine

radiator

fuel tank

**DID YOU KNOW?**

A car has 4 wheels but a truck can have 18!

# Aircraft

Hot-air balloons, gliders, aeroplanes, and helicopters are types of aircraft.

Aeroplanes use powerful engines and wings to climb into the air. They carry hundreds of thousands of people around the world every day. You may have been in one to go on your summer holidays.

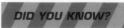
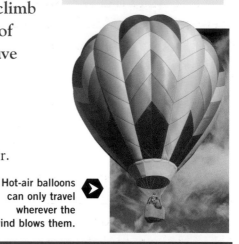

## Hot-air balloons

Hot-air balloons are filled with air. A burner heats the air. Hot air is lighter than the surrounding cold air. This makes the balloon float upwards. Most hot-air balloons have a basket that hangs underneath the balloon for people to stand in.

Hot-air balloons can only travel wherever the wind blows them.

## Airships

Airships are balloons with engines. The balloon usually contains helium gas, which is lighter than air. Airships can travel in any direction.

In the early 20th century, huge airships were the first aircraft to carry passengers long distances.

Another name for an airship is a dirigible.

## Helicopters

All helicopters have wings and an engine. A helicopter's wings are long and thin and are called blades. The blades spin round to lift the helicopter into the air.

 A coastguard helicopter on its way to carry out a rescue.

## Aeroplanes

Aeroplanes are streamlined. Streamlined shapes slip through the air easily.

All aeroplanes have wings. Slow planes have long wings that stick straight out sideways from the plane's body. Fast planes have wings that are arrow shaped.

## Lifting into the air

Aeroplanes weigh around 400 tonnes (440 tons) yet they can fly through the air. The shape of an aeroplane's wings make it fly.

When air flows across a wing, it makes the wing lift upwards and it carries the plane into the air. Planes need a tail as well as wings. The tail helps to keep the plane steady.

A glider is an aircraft with no engine. It is towed or winched into the air.

tail fin

air brakes

galley (kitchen)

wing

passenger seats

flaps can extend out to help the plane take off

flight deck

fuel tanks     jet engine

cargo hold (luggage section)

**DID YOU KNOW?**

The Harrier jump-jet doesn't need to travel along a runway to take off. It can take off and land vertically (straight up and down).

The parts of a jet aeroplane.

This eurofighter is a fighter plane. It can travel extremely fast and turn sharply in the air.

## Jet engines

An aeroplane's jet engine burns fuel and shoots out gases behind it. The gases force the plane to move forwards along a runway.

Most aeroplanes need a long runway to take off. The plane must travel between 240 kph (150 mph) and 290 kph (180 mph). Once in the air it can reach 885 kph (550 mph).

# Acknowledgements

*Edited by Harriet McGregor/Designed by Tinstar Design*

The publishers would like to thank the following for permission to use their material. Every care has been taken to trace copyright holders. However, if there have been unintentional omissions or failure to trace copyright holders, we apologise, and will, if informed, endeavour to make corrections in any future edition.

**Key**
t = top; b = bottom; c = centre; l = left; r = right; back = background; f = foreground

## Artwork

**Allington, Sophie:** 66b fore; 70t.

**Arlott, Norman:** 70cr.

**Baker, Julian:** 36cr; 113cr; 130br; 139c.

**Baum, Julian:** 94tr; 96b; 100cl.

**D'Achille, Gino:** 59br; 83cl; 89tr; 92tr; 94bl; 99tr; 102cr; 108tr; 110cr; 118tr; 131tr; 141tr; 152tr; 157tr; 159c.

**Farmer, Andrew:** 8br; 19r; 30br; 35b.

**Franklin, Mark:** 25bl; 30cl; 125cr; 126b; 141bl; 152bl; 153tr; 153bl; 158c; 174bl; 177 all.

**Full Steam Ahead:** 31br; 54t; 64br back; 86-87 back; 124bl.

**Gaffney, Michael:** 66b fore; 80bl.

**Gecko Ltd.:** 62br; 63tl; 154cl.

**Gulbis, Stephen:** 112c.

**Hardy, David:** 97c; 161tr.

**Hawken, Nick:** 101tr; 120bl.

**Hawtin, Nigel:** 61bl.

**Hincks, Gary:** 9b; 15cl; 16c; 22b; 23c; 31tr; 32cr; 38b.

**Hook, Richard:** 43b; 135tr.

**Jakeway, Rob:** 12b; 37b; 92l; 114tr; 114br; 129br; 165b; 166br.

**Kennard, Frank:** 40tr.

**Kent, Roger:** 17tl; 67c back; 68br; 172br.

**Learoyd, Tracey:** 14br; 21cr; 27cr; 35c; 57c; 85b; 136tr; 173b.

**Loates, Mick:** 71br; 82tr.

**Mendez, Simon/Sean Milne/Paul Richardson/Steve Roberts/Peter Visscher/Michael Woods:** 72-73b.

**Milne, Sean:** 18br; 85t.

**Milne, Sean/Paul Richardson/Steve Roberts/Peter Visscher:** 64br.

**Milne, Sean/Steve Roberts/Peter Visscher:** 66b fore; 86-87 fore.

**Ovendon, Dennis:** 88l.

**Oxford Illustrators:** 18bl; 109tr; 156tr; 178tr; 184b.

**Oxford University Press:** 15br; 29c.

**Parsley, Helen:** 55b (John Martin and Artists); 58cl; 89bl; 116c; 152cr; 169tr; 178br.

**Phoenix Mapping:** 122b.

**Polley, Robbie:** 148tr.

**Richardson, Paul:** 65tr; 81cr; 83cr.

**Riley, Terry:** 26cl; 62cr; 66t; 71bl; 81bl; 88cr.

**Roberts, Steve:** 42cr; 69tr; 73tr; 74tr; 75br; 76cl; 76b; 77 all; 84b.

**Sanders, Martin:** 69br.

**Sarson, Peter:** 151cl.

**Saunders, Michael:** 6cr; 7b; 11cr; 13c; 20cr; 27c; 33b; 36tl; 39b; 47c; 48b; 49bl; 50br; 51tr; 54b; 55tl; 90bl; 93c; 99tr; 134b; 138b; 140br; 143cl; 144c; 145br; 148cl; 168cl; 176c; 180 all.

**Smith, Guy:** 112r; 115r; 116tr; 116br; 118b; 127br; 155br.

**Sneddon, James:** 57tr; 105r; 123c; 162br.

**Stewart, Roger:** 145tr; 146c; 149tr; 181c; 185b; 187c.

**Visscher, Peter:** 8tr; 11br; 12cr; 24br; 45c; 48cl; 56tr; 71cl; 78br; 79cl; 87cr; 91tr; 103 all; 106tc; 107cr; 108br; 124tr; 125tr; 126c; 128tl; 133tr; 136bl; 137bl; 139tr; 144tr; 150c; 150bl; 159tr; 161br; 162tr; 164clb; 169br; 173tr; 181tr; 184tr; 186tr.

**Weston, Steve:** 44c; 45b; 49tr; 50cl; 50tr; 51br; 52b.

**Woods, Michael:** 17br; 24tr; 65c; 66b back; 80tr; 82bl; 82cr; 83bl; 131bl; 170cr; 171b.

## Photographs

Cover photos:

**Corbis:** Micro Discovery (back cover)

**OUP/Classet:** tr, br, cl

**Science Photo Library:** Andrew Syred (bl), Mehau Kulyk (front and back cover), Kenneth Libbrecht (tl)

Inside photos:

**Agco corporation:** 178bl

**Airbus S.A.S. 2007:** 180bl

**AKG- Images:** 156bl (Warner Bros. Pictures/Album/AK); 167tr (Dreamworks/Album)

**Brand X Pictures:** 186tr

**Corbis:** 10b (Roger Ressmeyer); 14tr (Lloyd Cluff); 14cl (Kontos Yannis); 15tr (Jim Sugar); 18tr (Frans Lanting); 20bl (Ralph White); 25tr (Eberhard Streichan/zefa); 39tr (Keren Su); 40cl (Reed Kaestner); 40br (Peter Beck); 41cl (Bob Daemmrich); 41br (Hubert Stadler); 43tr (Pierre Colombel); 44tr (Visuals Unlimited); 45tr; 47bl (Clouds Hill Imaging Ltd.); 48tr (Visuals Unlimited); 51cl (Redlink); 53tr (Gary Houlder); 58br (Ed Bock); 61tr; 63cr (Visuals

Unlimited); 72tr (Kevin Schafer); 74br (Michael & Patricia Fogden); 79tr (Mediscan); 80cl (Gary Braasch); 89cr (Roger Ressmeyer); 98tr (Dennis di Cicco); 100tr (Bettmann); 101bl (NASA TV/Handout/epa/Corbis); 102b (David Allio/Icon SMI); 108bl (Karl Staedele/dpa); 109br (Jo Lillini); 117tr (Roy McMahon); 121tr (Kim Kulish); 125bl (Visuals Unlimited); 129tr (George Hall); 131cr (Soltan Frederic); 132cr (Kevin R. Morris); 148br (Jose Fuste Raga); 149br (Du Huaju/Xinhua Press); 151tr (Archivo Iconografico, S.A.); 151bl (Construction Photography); 152br (Clouds Hill Imaging Ltd); 155c (Bernd Settnik/dpa); 157br; 158bl (Gideon Mendel); 159bc (James Leynse); 163bl; 168tr (Ingo Wagner/epa); 168br (Yuriko Nakao/Reuters); 172tr (Vince Streano); 173cr (Liu Liqun); 176bl (Bettmann); 179cl; 179cr; 181bl (Wulf Pfeiffer/dpa/epa); 182cr (Qilai Shen/epa); 185tr (Tim Wright); 187bl (Paco Campos/EFE)

**Digital Vision:** 29bc, 33tl, 37tr, 42tl, 130cl, 135bl; 172cl; 175tr; 177tr; 182bl

**Getty Images:** 22tl (Paul Chesley); 36bl (Arnulf Husmo); 141cr (Peter Ginter); 143tr (Gabriel M Covian); 160cl (Evan Agostini)

**Google Inc.:** 168tr

**Haddon Davies:** 91br; 110tr; 111r

**IBM:** 150br

**Istockphoto:** 7cr (Roman Krochuk); 8cl (Edward Todd); 9tc (David Gilder); 9tr (Matthew Scherf); 11tr (Joseph Hoyle); 12cl (Emrah Turudu); 13tr (Tomasz Resiak); 16tr (John Woodworth); 19br (David Mathies); 20br (Chris Ronneseth); 21tr (Henk Badenhorst); 23br (Elena Korenbaum); 27bl (Joe Gough); 28tr (Trientje Jeanette); 31cl (Marc C. Johnson); 34tl (Clint Spencer); 34c (Nico Smit); 34br (Franky De Meyer); 38tr (Daniel Stein); 41tr (Rafa Irusta); 46tr (Gordana Sermek); 46cl (Michael Lynch); 46br (Misha Shiyanov); 54c (Carmen Martínez Banús); 56bl (Jim Kolaczko); 57bl (Galina Barskaya); 59bl (Dagmara Ponikiewska); 65bl (jamesbenet); 68tl (Bernd Heusing); 69cl (Armin Rose); 70bl (Beverley Vycital); 71tr (Anthony Hall); 73bl (Johan Swanepoel); 79br (marmion); 80br (John Pitcher); 90tr (Thomas Tuchan); 94br (Michael Puerzer); 95bl; 104br (Alexander Hafemann); 106cl; 108br (Marek Pawluczuk); 107br (Richard Hawkes); 111bl (Francisco Neri); 112bl; 113tr; 114l (Auke Holwerda); 117bl (Artur Achtelik); 119br (Anthony Brown); 120br; 124tl (Lisa Kyle Young); 127bl (Samuel Kessler); 128cl (Chris Meadows); 128br (Manfred Karner); 129cl (Dan Brandenburg); 132cl (Steven Stone); 133cr (Shaun Lowe); 136cr; 137tr; 139br (David H. Lewis); 140tr (Peter Mleku); 142tr; 142br (Nancy Louie); 143cr (Vasko Miokovic); 145bl; 146bl (Teun Van Den); 149cl (Kathy Steen); 157cl (Brian Stanback); 160br; 163cr (Igor Karon); 164tr (Nicholas Monu); 170tr (Przemyslaw Rzeszutko); 170bl (Rainer Hillebran); 171cl (Randy Jeide); 179tr; 186bl (Stephen Finn); 187tr (Pete Masson)

**Mary Evans Picture Library:** 10tr

**Michelin:** 144tl

**NASA:** 30tr, 32cl, 91cl, 94cr (GSFC/METI/ERSDAC/JAROS, and U.S./Japan ASTER Science Team); 96cl, 98cl (The Hubble Heritage Team (AURA/STScI/NASA)); 98br (ESA, and the Hubble Heritage Team (STScI/ AURA)-ESA/Hubble Collaboration); 99cr (R. Williams); 100br; 120tr; 123tr; 153cr (Brad Whitmore (STScI))

**NHPA:** 17cr (John Shaw)

**NOAA:** 6b (NGDC/Peter W. Sloss); 28bl

**Oxford Scientific Films:** 24bl (Carol Farneti Partridge Films Ltd.); 26tr (Carol Farneti Partridge Films Ltd.); 75tr (Mark Deeble & Victoria Stone); 81tl (Animals Animals / Earth Scenes); 83tr (Joe McDonald/AA); 84tr (Densey Clyne); 133cl (Animals Animals/Earth Scenes); 156br (Stephen Downer)

**Photodisc:** 6t; 96cr; 110bl; 113bl

**Photolibrary:** 107cl (Aflo Foto Agency)

**Science Photo Library:** 20tr (Baerbel K. Luccitta/US Geological Survey), 56cr (A. Crump, TDR, WHO); 59tr (Matt Meadows, Peter Arnold Inc.); 60tr (BSIP LECA); 60br (Simon Fraser); 60bc inset (Moredun Animal Health Ltd.); 63bl (Nancy Kedersha); 119bl (Alex Bartel); 138tr; 140cl (R. Maisonneuve, Publiphoto Diffusion); 154tr (Novastock); 154bl (William Ervin); 162cl (Dr Jeremy Burgess); 167cl (Maximilian Stock Ltd); 167br (NASA); 169bl (Geoff Tompkinson)

**Shutterstock:** 58tr; 77br (Brian Finestone), 105l (EuToch); 115bl (Ramon Berk); 116bl (Kenn Stilger); 121bl (VisualField); 122tr (Graham S. Klotz); 126tr (Karl R. Martin); 127tr (Vaclav Mach); 130tr (Tihis); 132tr (Alexei Novikov); 134tr (ARTEKI); 135cr (Sagasan); 137c (Graham Tomlin); 155tr (Christoph Weihs); 155bl (TEA); 160tr (foto.fritz); 161bl (Olaru Radian-Alexandru); 164cl (Filipchuk Oleg Vasiliovich); 164bl (Norman Chan); 171tr (Rui Manuel Teles Gomes); 175cl (Chad McDermott); 175br (Daniel Goodings); 183bl (Keith Robinson); 184cr (digitalsport-photoagency); 186cr (Bateleur)

**Specialized bicycles:** 183tl

**Virgin Atlantic:** 163tl

# Index

Page numbers in **bold** mean that this is where you will find the most information on that subject. If both a heading and a page number are in bold, there is an article with that title. A page number in *italic* means that there is a picture of that subject. There may also be other information about the subject on the same page.